THE

HARP AND THE CROSS:

A

COLLECTION OF RELIGIOUS POETRY,

COMPILED BY

STEPHEN G. BULFINCH.

"Spirit of God! whose glory once o'erhung
A throne, the ark's dread cherubim between,
So let thy presence brood, though now unseen,
O'er those two powers by whom the harp is strung,
Feeling and Thought! — till the rekindled chords
Give the long-buried tone back to immortal words!"
HEMANS.

THIRD EDITION.

BOSTON:
WALKER, WISE, AND COMPANY,
245 WASHINGTON STREET.
1861.

University Press, Cambridge:
Electrotyped and Printed by Welch, Bigelow, & Co.

NOTICE.

In preparing this collection of religious poetry, the attempt has been made to meet the various occasions which suggest devout thought. The compiler has found pleasure in presenting specimens from writers in the same communion with himself; but piety and genius have been welcomed from every source. The different productions have been arranged upon a general plan, commencing with the lessons which Nature teaches, and ascending to the highest anticipations of Christian faith.

The work, undertaken at the request of the Executive Committee of the American Unitarian Association, has been adopted as one of their series of books entitled *The Devotional Library*. Four volumes in this series are now published, to wit: — Vol. I. The Altar at Home; Vol. II. The Christian Doctrine of Prayer, by Rev. J. F. Clarke; Vol. III. The Rod and the Staff, by Rev. T. T. Stone; Vol. IV. The Harp and the Cross, by Rev. S. G. Bulfinch.

CONTENTS.

PART I.

NATURE.

PART II.

REVELATION: THE OLD TESTAMENT.

PART III.

THE GOSPEL.

PART IV.

MEDITATION, PRAYER, AND PRAISE.

PART V.

ACTIVE DUTY.

PART VI.

PENITENCE.

PART VII.

TRUST AND SUBMISSION.

PART VIII.

DEATH AND IMMORTALITY.

PART I.

NATURE.

MORNING HYMN OF A HERMIT.

JOHN STERLING.

Sweet Morn! from countless cups of gold
  Thou liftest reverently on high
More incense fine than earth can hold,
    To fill the sky.

One interfusion wide of love,
  Thine airs and odors moist ascend,
And, 'mid the azure depths above,
    With light they blend.

The lark, by his own carol blest,
  From the green harbors eager springs;
And his large heart in little breast
    Exulting sings.

On lands and seas, on fields and woods,
And cottage roofs and ancient spires,
O Morn! thy gaze creative broods,
While Night retires.

Aloft, the mountain ridges beam
Above their quiet steeps of gray;
The eastern clouds with glory stream.
And vital day.

By valleys dank, and river's brim,
Through corn-clad fields and wizard groves,
O'er dazzling tracks and hollows dim,
One spirit roves.

The broad-helmed oak-tree's endless growth,
The mossy stone that crowns the hill,
The violet's breast, to gazers loath,
In sunshine thrill.

A joy from hidden paradise
Is rippling down the shiny brooks,
With beauty like the gleams of eyes
In tenderest looks.

Where'er the vision's boundaries glance,
Existence swells with teeming power,
And all illumined earth's expanse
Inhales the hour.

Not sands, and rocks, and seas immense,
  And vapors thin, and halls of air, —
Not these alone, with kindred glance,
        The splendor share.

The fly his jocund round inweaves,
  With choral strain the birds salute
The voiceful flocks, and nothing grieves,
        And naught is mute.

In Man, O Morn! a loftier good,
  With conscious blessing, fills the soul,
A life by reason understood,
        Which metes the whole.

With healthful pulse, and tranquil fire,
  Which plays at ease in every limb,
His thoughts unchecked to heaven aspire,
        Revealed in him.

To thousand tasks of fruitful hope,
  With skill against his toil he bends,
And finds his work's determined scope
        Where'er he wends.

From earth, and earthly toil and strife,
  To deathless aims his love may rise;
Each dawn may wake to better life,
        With purer eyes.

Such grace from thee, O God! be ours,
Renewed with every morning's ray,
And freshening still with added flowers
Each future day.

To Man is given one primal star;
One day-spring's beam has dawned below.
From Thine our inmost glories are,
With Thine we glow.

Like earth, awake, and warm and bright
With joy, the spirit moves and burns;
So up to thee, O Fount of Light!
Our light returns.

MORNING THOUGHTS.

MARY HOWITT.

The summer sun is shining
Upon a world so bright!
The dew upon each grassy blade,
The golden light, the depth of shade,
All seem as they were only made
To minister delight.

From giant trees, strong branched,
  And all their veiny leaves,
From little birds that madly sing,
From insects fluttering on the wing,
Ay, from the very meanest thing,
  My spirit joy receives.

I think of angel voices
  When the birds' songs I hear;
Of that celestial city, bright
With jacinth, gold, and chrysolite,
When with its blazing pomp of light
  The morning doth appear.

I think of that great river
  That from the throne flows free,
Of weary pilgrims on its brink,
Who, thirsting, have come down to drink;
Of that unfailing stream I think
  When earthly streams I see.

I think of pain and dying,
  As that which is but naught,
When glorious morning, warm and bright,
With all its voices of delight,
From the chill darkness of the night,
  Like a new life, is brought.

I think of human sorrow
 But as of clouds that brood
Upon the bosom of the day,
And the next moment pass away;
And with a trusting heart I say,
 Thank God, *all things are good!*

THE WANDERER'S ADORATION.

FROM "THE EXCURSION." — WILLIAM WORDSWORTH.

How beautiful this dome of sky,
And the vast hills in fluctuation fixed
At Thy command, how awful! Shall the Soul,
Human and rational, report of Thee
Even less than these? Be mute who will, who can,
Yet I will praise Thee with impassioned voice:
My lips, that may forget Thee in the crowd,
Cannot forget Thee here; where Thou hast built,
For thy own glory, in the wilderness!
Me didst Thou constitute a priest of thine,
In such a temple as we now behold
Reared for thy presence: therefore am I bound
To worship, here and everywhere, as one
Not doomed to ignorance, though forced to tread,
From childhood up, the ways of poverty;
From unreflecting ignorance preserved,

And from debasement rescued. By Thy grace
The particle divine remained unquenched;
And, 'mid the wild weeds of a rugged soil,
Thy bounty caused to flourish deathless flowers,
From Paradise transplanted: wintry age
Impends; the frost will gather round my heart;
If the flowers wither, I am worse than dead!
Come, Labor, when the worn-out frame requires
Perpetual sabbath; come, disease and want;
And sad exclusion through decay of sense;
But leave me unabated trust in Thee, —
And let thy favor, to the end of life,
Inspire me with ability to seek
Repose and hope among eternal things, —
Father of heaven and earth! and I am rich,
And will possess my portion in content.

A SABBATH SUMMER NOON.

AN EXTRACT.

WILLIAM MOTHERWELL.

THE calmness of this noontide hour,
  The shadow of this wood,
The fragrance of each wilding flower,
  Are marvellously good;
O, here crazed spirits breathe the balm
  Of nature's solitude!

It is a most delicious calm
  That resteth everywhere, —
The holiness of soul-sung psalm,
  Of felt but voiceless prayer!
With hearts too full to speak their bliss,
  God's creatures silent are.

They silent are; but not the less,
  In this most tranquil hour
Of deep unbroken dreaminess,
  They own that Love and Power
Which, like the softest sunshine, rests
  On every leaf and flower.

How silent are the song-filled nests
  That crowd this drowsy tree!
How mute is every feathered breast
  That swelled with melody!
And yet bright, bead-like eyes declare
  This hour is ecstasy.

Heart forth! as uncaged bird through air,
  And mingle in the tide
Of blessed things, that, lacking care,
  Now full of beauty glide
Around thee, in their angel hues
  Of joy and sinless pride.

Here, on this green bank that o'erviews
  The far-retreating glen,

Beneath the spreading beech-tree muse
  On all within thy ken;
For lovelier scene shall never break
  On thy dimmed sight again.

Slow stealing through the tangled brake
  That skirts the distant hill,
With noiseless hoof two bright fawns make
  For yonder lapsing rill;
Meek children of the forest gloom,
  Drink on, and fear no ill!

. . . . .

I bend me towards the tiny flower,
  That underneath this tree
Opens its little breast of sweets
  In meekest modesty,
And breathes the eloquence of love,
  In muteness, Lord! to thee.

. . . . .

Far down the glen in distance gleams
  The hamlet's tapering spire,
And glittering in meridial beams,
  Its vane is tongued with fire;
And hark how sweet its silvery bell,
  And hark the rustic choir!

The holy sounds float up the dell
  To fill my ravished ear,
And now the glorious anthems swell
  Of worshippers sincere,—

Of hearts bowed in the dust, that shed
  Faith's penitential tear.

Dear Lord! thy shadow is forth spread
  On all mine eye can see;
And, filled at the pure fountain-head
  Of deepest piety,
My heart loves all created things,
  And travels home to thee.

Around me while the sunshine flings
  A flood of mocky gold,
My chastened spirit once more sings,
  As it was wont of old,
That lay of gratitude which burst
  From young heart uncontrolled,

When, in the midst of nature nursed,
  Sweet influences fell
On childly hearts that were athirst,
  Like soft dews in the bell
Of tender flowers, that bowed their heads,
  And breathed a fresher smell.

So, even now this hour hath sped
  In rapturous thought o'er me,
Feeling myself with nature wed, —
  A holy mystery, —
A part of earth, a part of heaven,
  A part, great God! of thee.

THE USE OF FLOWERS.

MARY HOWITT.

God might have made the earth bring forth
Enough for great and small,
The oak-tree and the cedar-tree,
Without a flower at all.

We might have had enough, enough
For every want of ours,
For luxury, medicine, and toil,
And yet have had no flowers.

The ore within the mountain mine
Requireth none to grow;
Nor doth it need the lotus-flower
To make the river flow.

The clouds might give abundant rain,
The nightly dews might fall,
And the herb that keepeth life in man,
Might yet have drunk them all.

Then wherefore, wherefore were they made,
All dyed with rainbow light,
All fashioned with supremest grace
Upspringing day and night, —

Springing in valleys green and low,
And on the *mountains high,*
And in the silent wilderness
Where no man passes by?

Our outward life requires them not;
Then wherefore had they birth?—
To minister delight to man,
To beautify the earth.

To comfort man,—to whisper hope
Whene'er his faith is dim;
For who so careth for the flowers
Will much more care for him!

THE WOODLAND SANCTUARY

F. D. HUNTINGTON.

O Thou, that once on Horeb stood
Revealed within the burning tree,
To-day, as well, in each green wood,
Be seen by hearts that yearn for thee.
Each shining leaf is bright with God,
Each bough a prophet's "budding rod,"
Each by thy flaming sun illumed,
Yet each, like Horeb's, unconsumed.

O Thou, whose hand poured Jordan's stream,
Whose angel-dove hung o'er its wave,
To hallow with a heavenly gleam
The Son whose love a world would save!
Bring from the waters at our side
Some whisper, gentle as their tide,
Saying, like Christ on Galilee, —
That holier lake, — Peace, peace to thee!

We pray, O Lord, who touched the mount, —
We pray through Him who stilled the sea, —
May every outward sight a fount
Of inward life and courage be.
The radiant bush, the white-winged dove,
The fire of faith, the peace of love,
Uplift our souls, and urge them on
To take the cross, to wear the crown.

SCENE AFTER A SUMMER SHOWER.

ANDREWS NORTON.

The rain is o'er. How dense and bright
Yon pearly clouds reposing lie, —
Cloud above cloud, a glorious sight,
Contrasting with the dark blue sky!

In grateful silence, earth receives
  The general blessing; fresh and fair,
Each flower expands its little leaves,
  As glad the common joy to share.

The softened sunbeams pour around
  A fairy light, uncertain, pale;
The wind flows cool; the scented ground
  Is breathing odors on the gale.

'Mid yon rich cloud's voluptuous pile,
  Methinks some spirit of the air
Might rest, to gaze below awhile,
  Then turn to bathe and revel there.

The sun breaks forth; from off the scene
  Its floating veil of mist is flung;
And all the wilderness of green
  With trembling drops of light is hung.

Now gaze on Nature, — yet the same,
  Glowing with life, by breezes fanned,
Luxuriant, lovely, as she came,
  Fresh in her youth, from God's own hand.

Hear the rich music of that voice
  Which sounds from all below, above
She calls her children to rejoice,
  And round them throws her arms of love.

Drink in her influence; low-born care,
And all the train of mean desire,
Refuse to breathe this holy air,
And 'mid this living light expire.

THE PASTOR'S PRAYER AT SUNSET.

FROM "THE EXCURSION." — WILLIAM WORDSWORTH.

"Eternal Spirit! universal God!
Power inaccessible to human thought,
Save by degrees and steps which Thou hast deigned
To furnish; for this effluence of thyself,
To the infirmity of mortal sense
Vouchsafed, — this local transitory type
Of thy paternal splendors, and the pomp
Of those who fill thy courts in highest heaven,
The radiant Cherubim, — accept the thanks
Which we, thy humble creatures, here convened,
Presume to offer; we, who, from the breast
Of the frail earth permitted to behold
The faint reflections only of thy face,
Are yet exalted, and in soul adore!
Such as they are who in thy presence stand

Unsullied, incorruptible, and drink
Imperishable majesty streamed forth
From thy empyreal throne, the elect of earth
Shall be, — divested at the appointed hour
Of all dishonor, cleansed from mortal stain.
— Accomplish, then, their number; and conclude
Time's weary course! Or if, by thy decree,
The consummation that will come by stealth
Be yet far distant, let thy Word prevail, —
Oh! let thy Word prevail, to take away
The sting of human nature. Spread the Law,
As it is written in thy holy Book,
Throughout all lands: let every nation hear
The high behest, and every heart obey;
Both for the love of purity, and hope
Which it affords, to such as do thy will
And persevere in good, that they shall rise,
To have a nearer view of Thee, in heaven.
— Father of Good! this prayer in bounty grant,
In mercy grant it to thy wretched sons.
Then, nor till then, shall persecution cease,
And cruel wars expire. The way is marked,
The Guide appointed, and the ransom paid.
Alas! the nations who of yore received
These tidings, and in Christian temples meet
The sacred truth to acknowledge, linger still;
Preferring bonds and darkness to a state
Of holy freedom, by redeeming love
Proffered to all, while yet on earth detained.

. . . . .

"Once," and with mild demeanor, as he spake,
On us the venerable Pastor turned
His beaming eye that had been raised to Heaven, —
"Once, while the name Jehovah was a sound
Within the circuit of this sea-girt isle
Unheard, the savage nations bowed the head
To gods delighting in remorseless deeds;
Gods which themselves had fashioned, to promote
Ill purposes, and flatter foul desires.
Then, in the bosom of yon mountain cove
To those inventions of corrupted man
Mysterious rites were solemnized; and there,
Amid impending rocks and gloomy woods,
Of those terrific Idols some received
Such dismal service, that the loudest voice
Of the swoln cataracts (which now are heard
Soft murmuring) was too weak to overcome,
Though aided by wild winds, the groans and shrieks
Of human victims, offered up to appease
Or to propitiate. And, if living eyes
Had visionary faculties to see
The thing that hath been as the thing that is,
Aghast we might behold this crystal Mere
Bedimmed with smoke, in wreaths voluminous,
Flung from the body of devouring fires,
To Taranis erected on the heights

By priestly hands, for sacrifice performed
Exultingly, in view of open day
And full assemblage of a barbarous host;
Or to Andates, female Power! who gave
(For so they fancied) glorious victory.
— A few rude monuments of mountain stone
Survive; all else is swept away. — How bright
The appearances of things! From such, how changed
The existing worship; and with those compared,
The worshippers how innocent and blest!
So wide the difference, a willing mind,
At this affecting hour, might almost think
That Paradise, the lost abode of man,
Was raised again; and to a happy few,
In its original beauty, here restored.

"Whence but from Thee, the true and only God,
And from the faith derived through Him who bled
Upon the Cross, this marvellous advance
Of good from evil? as if one extreme
Were left, the other gained. — O ye, who come
To kneel devoutly in yon reverend Pile,
Called to such office by the peaceful sound
Of Sabbath bells; and ye, who sleep in earth,
All cares forgotten, round its hallowed walls!
For you, in presence of this little band
Gathered together on the green hill-side,
Your Pastor is emboldened to prefer

Vocal thanksgivings to the Eternal King;
Whose love, whose counsel, whose commands, have made
Your very poorest rich in peace of thought
And in good works; and him who is endowed
With scantiest knowledge, master of all truth
Which the salvation of his soul requires.
Conscious of that abundant favor showered
On you, the children of my humble care,
And this dear land, our country while on earth
We sojourn, have I lifted up my soul,
Joy giving voice to fervent gratitude.
These barren rocks, your stern inheritance;
These fertile fields, that recompense your pains;
The shadowy vale, the sunny mountain top;
Woods waving in the wind their lofty heads,
Or hushed; the roaring waters, and the still; —
They see the offering of my lifted hands,
They hear my lips present their sacrifice,
They know if I be silent, morn or even:
For, though in whispers speaking, the full heart
Will find a vent; and thought is praise to Him,
Audible praise to Thee, Omniscient Mind,
From whom all gifts descend, all blessings flow!"

EVENTIDE.

WRITTEN IN THE COUNTRY.

J. T. FIELDS.

THIS cottage door, this gentle gale,
Hay-scented, whispering round,
Yon path-side rose, that down the vale
Breathes incense from the ground,
Methinks should from the dullest clod
Invite a thankful heart to God.

But, Lord, the violet, bending low,
Seems better moved to praise;
From us, what scanty blessings flow,
How voiceless close our days!
Father, forgive us, and the flowers
Shall lead in prayer the vesper hours.

THE EVENING HYMN.

THOMAS MILLER.

How many days, with mute adieu,
Have gone down yon untrodden sky!
And still it looks as clear and blue
As when it first was hung on high.

The rolling sun, the frowning cloud
  That drew the lightning in its rear,
The thunder, tramping deep and loud,
  Have left no footmark there.

The village bells, with silver chime,
  Come softened by the distant shore;
Though I have heard them many a time,
  They never rung so sweet before.
A silence rests upon the hill,
  A listening awe pervades the air;
The very flowers are shut, and still,
  And bowed as if in prayer.

And in this hushed and breathless close,
  O'er earth, and air, and sky, and sea,
That still low voice in silence goes,
  Which speaks alone, great God, of Thee.
The whispering leaves, the far-off brook,
  The linnet's warble fainter grown,
The hive-bound bee, the lonely rook,—
  All these their Maker own.

Now shine the starry hosts of light,
  Gazing on earth with golden eyes;
Bright guardians of the blue-browed night,
  What are ye in your native skies?
I know not! neither can I know,
  Nor on what leader ye attend,

Nor whence ye came, nor whither go,
  Nor what your aim, or end.

I know they must be holy things,
  That from a room so sacred shine,
Where sounds the beat of angel-wings,
  And footsteps echo all divine.
Their mysteries I never sought,
  Nor hearkened to what science tells;
For, oh! in childhood I was taught
  That God amidst them dwells.

The darkening woods, the fading trees,
  The grasshopper's last feeble sound,
The flower just wakened by the breeze,
  All leave the stillness more profound.
The twilight takes a deeper shade,
  The dusky path-ways blacker grow,
And silence reigns in glen and glade,—
  All, all is mute below.

And other eves as sweet as this
  Will close upon as calm a day,
And, sinking down the deep abyss,
  Will, like the last, be swept away;
Until Eternity is gained,
  That boundless sea without a shore,
That without Time for ever reigned,
  And will when Time 's no more.

Now nature sinks in soft repose,
  A living semblance of the grave;
The dew steals noiseless on the rose,
  The boughs have almost ceased to wave;
The silent sky, the sleeping earth,
  Tree, mountain stream, the humble sod,
All tell from whom they had their birth,
  And cry, "Behold a God!"

EVENING SONG OF THE WEARY.

MRS. HEMANS.

FATHER of Heaven and Earth!
    I bless thee for the night,
    The soft, still night!
The holy pause of care and mirth,
    Of sound and light!

Now far in glade and dell,
Flower-cup, and bud, and bell
Have shut around the sleeping woodlark's nest;
The bee's long murmuring toils are done,
And I, the o'erwearied one,
O'erwearied and o'erwrought,
Bless thee, O God, O Father of the oppressed,
With my last waking thought,
    In the still night!

Yes, ere I sink to rest,
By the fire's dying light,
Thou Lord of Earth and Heaven!
I bless thee, who hast given
Unto life's fainting travellers the night,—
The soft, still, holy night!

THE RISING MOON.

W. B. O. PEABODY.

The moon is up! how calm and slow
She wheels above the hill!
The weary winds forget to blow,
And all the world lies still.

The way-worn travellers with delight
Her rising brightness see,
Revealing all the paths and plains,
And gilding every tree.

It glistens where the hurrying stream
Its little rippling heaves;
It falls upon the forest-shade,
And sparkles on the leaves.

So once on Judah's evening hills
The heavenly lustre spread;
The Gospel sounded from the blaze,
And shepherds gazed with dread.

And still that light upon the world
Its guiding splendor throws,
Bright in the opening hours of life,
And brighter at its close.

The waning moon in time shall fail
To walk the midnight skies;
But God hath kindled this bright light
With fire that never dies.

THE LIGHT OF STARS.

W. H. FURNESS.

Slowly, by God's hand unfurled,
Down around the weary world
Falls the darkness: O how still
Is the working of His will!

Mighty Spirit, ever nigh!
Work in me as silently;
Veil the day's distracting sights,
Show me heaven's eternal lights.

Living stars to view be brought,
In the boundless realms of thought;
High and infinite desires,
Flaming like those upper fires!

Holy Truth, eternal Right, —
Let them break upon my sight;
Let them shine serene and still,
And with light my being fill.

THE INFINITY OF SPACE.

JOHN STERLING.

When up to nightly skies we gaze,
Where stars pursue their endless ways,
We think we see from earth's low clod
The wide and shining home of God.

But could we rise to moon or sun,
Or path where planets duly run,
Still heaven would spread above us far,
And earth remote would seem a star.

'T is vain to dream those tracts of space
With all their worlds approach His face;
One glory fills each wheeling ball, —
One love has shaped and moved them all.

This earth, with all its dust and tears,
Is His no less than yonder spheres;
And rain-drops weak, and grains of sand
Are stamped by His immediate hand.

The rock, the wave, the little flower,
All fed by streams of living power,
That spring from one Almighty will,
Whate'er His thought conceives, fulfil.

And is this all that man can claim?
Is this our longing's final aim?
To be like all things round, — no more
Than pebbles cast on Time's gray shore?

Can man, no more than beast, aspire
To know his being's awful Sire?
And, born and lost on Nature's breast,
No blessing seek but there to rest?

Not this our doom, thou God benign!
Whose rays on us unclouded shine:
Thy breath sustains yon fiery dome;
But man is most thy favored home.

We view those halls of painted air,
And own Thy presence makes them fair;
But dearer still to thee, O Lord!
Is he whose thoughts to thine accord.

MELODIES AND MYSTERIES.

CHARLES MACKAY.

WOULDST thou know what the blithe bird pipeth
High in the morning air?
Wouldst thou know what the blithe stream singeth,
Rippling o'er pebbles bare?
Sorrow the mystery shall teach thee
And the words declare.

Wouldst thou find in the rose's blossom
More than thy fellows find?
More in the fragrance of the lily
Than odor on the wind?
Love Nature, and her smallest atoms
Shall whisper to thy mind.

Wouldst thou know what the moon discourseth
To the docile sea?
Wouldst hear the echoes of the music
Of the far infinity!
Sorrow shall ope the founts of knowledge,
And heaven shall sing to thee.

Wouldst thou see through the riddle of Being
Further than others can?

Sorrow shall give thine eyes new lustre
    To simplify the plan;
And love of God and thy kind shall aid thee
    To end what it began.

To Love and Sorrow all Nature speaketh;
    If the riddle be read,
They the best can see through darkness
    Each divergent tread
Of its mazy texture, and discover
    Whence the ravel spread.

Love and Sorrow are sympathetic
    With the earth and skies;
Their touch from the harp of Nature bringeth
    The hidden melodies;
To them the eternal chords for ever
    Vibrate in harmonies.

CORRESPONDENCES.

C. P. CRANCH.

All things in Nature are beautiful types to the
    soul that will read them;
Nothing exists upon earth, but for unspeakable
    ends.

Every object that speaks to the senses was meant
for the spirit:
Nature is but a scroll, — God's handwriting
thereon.
Ages ago, when man was pure, ere the flood
overwhelmed him,
While in the image of God every soul yet
lived,
Everything stood as a letter or word of a language familiar,
Telling of truths which *now* only the angels can
read.
Lost to man was the key of those sacred hieroglyphics, —
Stolen away by sin, — till with Jesus restored.
Now with infinite pains we here and there spell
out a letter;
Now and then will the sense feebly shine through
the dark.
When we perceive the light which breaks through
the visible symbol,
What exultation is ours! *we* the discovery have
made!
Yet is the meaning the same as when Adam
lived sinless in Eden,
Only long-hidden it slept, and now again is restored.
Man unconsciously uses figures of speech every
moment,

Little dreaming the cause why to such terms he is prone, —
Little dreaming that everything has its own correspondence
Folded within it of old, as in the body the soul.
Gleams of the mystery fall on us still, though much is forgotten,
And through our commonest speech illumines the path of our thoughts.
Thus does the lordly sun shine out a type of the Godhead;
Wisdom and Love the beams that shine on a darkened world.
Thus do the sparkling waters flow, giving joy to the desert,
And the great Fountain of Life opens itself to the thirst.
Thus does the word of God distil like the rain and the dew-drops,
Thus does the warm wind breathe like to the Spirit of God,
And the green grass and the flowers are signs of the regeneration.

O thou Spirit of Truth! visit our minds once more!
Give us to read, in letters of light, the language celestial,

Written all over the earth, — written all over the sky;
Thus may we bring our hearts at length to know our Creator,
Seeing in all things around types of the Infinite Mind.

NIAGARA.

JOHN G. C. BRAINARD.

The thoughts are strange that crowd into my brain
While I look upward to thee! It would seem
As if God poured thee from his hollow hand,
And hung his bow upon thine awful front,
And spoke in that loud voice, which seemed to him
Who dwelt in Patmos for his Saviour's sake,
"The sound of many waters," and had bade
Thy flood to chronicle the ages back,
And notch His centuries in the eternal rocks.

Deep calleth unto deep, — and what are we
That hear the question of that voice sublime?
O, what are all the notes that ever rung

From war's vain trumpet, by thy thundering side?
Yea, what is all the riot man can make,
In his short life, to thine unceasing roar?
And yet, bold babbler, what art thou to Him
Who drowned the world, and heaped the waters
far
Above its loftiest mountains? A light wave,
That breaks and whispers of his Maker's might!

THE BACKWOODSMAN.

EPHRAIM PEABODY.

The silent wilderness for me!
Where never sound is heard,
Save the rustling of the squirrel's foot
And the flitting wing of bird,
Or its low and interrupted note,
And the deer's quick, crackling tread,
And the swaying of the forest boughs,
As the wind moves overhead.

Alone, — how glorious to be free! —
My good dog at my side,
My rifle hanging on my arm,
I range the forests wide.

And now the regal buffalo
  Across the plains I chase;
Now track the mountain stream, to find
  The beaver's lurking-place.

I stand upon the mountain's top,
  And—solitude profound!—
Not even a woodman's smoke curls up
  Within the horizon's bound.
Below, as o'er its ocean breadth
  The air's light currents run,
The wilderness of moving leaves
  Is glancing in the sun.

I look around to where the sky
  Meets the far forest line,
And this imperial domain,
  This kingdom, all is mine!
This bending heaven, these floating clouds,
  Waters that ever roll,
And wilderness of glory, bring
  Their offerings to my soul.

My palace, built by God's own hand,
  The world's fresh prime hath seen;
Wide stretch its living halls away,
  Pillared and roofed with green.
My music is the wind that now
  Pours loud its swelling bars,

Now lulls in dying cadences;
  My festal lamps are stars.

Though when, in this my lonely home,
  My star-watched couch I press,
I hear no fond "Good night!" think not
  I am companionless.
O no! I see my father's house,
  The hill, the tree, the stream,
And the looks and voices of my home
  Come gently to my dream.

And in the solitary haunts,
  While slumbers every tree,
In night and silence, God himself
  Seems nearer unto me.
I *feel* his presence in the shades,
  Like the embracing air;
And as my eyelids close in sleep,
  My heart is hushed in prayer.

LINES WRITTEN AT TOCCOA FALLS, GEORGIA.

S. G. BULFINCH.

  Loveliest and most sublime!
Flashing in virgin whiteness from the skies!
Here may the traveller fix his raptured eyes,
  Nor heed quick-passing time.

Through thy transparent veil,
And wide around thee, Nature's grandest forms,
Rocks, built for ages to abide the storms,
Frown on the subject dale.

Fed by thy rapid stream,
In every crevice of that savage pile
The living herbs in quiet beauty smile,
Lit by the sunny gleam.

And over all, that gush
Of rain-drops, brightly sparkling in the sun!
While ages round thee on their course have run,
Forever on they rush.

I would not that the bow
With gorgeous hues should light thy virgin stream;
Better thy white and sunlit foam should gleam
Thus, like pure mountain snow.

Yes! thou hast seen these woods
Around, for centuries, rise, decay, and die,
While thou hast poured thine endless current by
To join the eternal floods.

The ages pass away;
Successive nations rise and are forgot,
But on thy brilliant course thou pausest not, —
Thy changing, changeless play.

When I have sunk to rest,
Thus wilt thou pass, in calm sublimity.
Then be thy voice to others, as to me,
To the deep soul addressed.

Here does a spirit dwell
Of gratitude and contemplation high,
Holding deep union with eternity.
O loveliest scene, farewell!

TONGUES.

A. D. T. W.

" And every man heard them in his own language."

Earth speaks to us! Her seasons, as they roll,
Give noble utterings,
And inward bear sweet influence o'er the soul,—
Summers and springs!

Life hath its lessons, — fervent love, and losing,
Rapture and pain,
Writ on the leaf that turns not at our choosing,
Nor turns in vain.

And every earnest spirit finds a tongue,
A mystic tone

Out on an air of mingled echoes flung,
Seeking its own.

God speaketh! He hath left beyond the sky
His awful crown,
And, wearing lesser robes of majesty,
To earth comes down.

Take heed how ye shall hear,—in gratitude,
Coldness, or scorn,—
Since to each soul that tongue is understood,
Wherein 't is born.

Art thou alive to things of sense alone?
Then shalt thou hear,
Naught else, though heaven and earth their thunder tone
Shout in thine ear.

Dost reverent wait and listen for the teaching
From all things given?
Then doth thine attitude of pure beseeching
Lift thee to heaven!

A voice shall one day utter weal or woe
To souls of men,
And "each in his own language," learned below,
Must hear it then!

THE LILIES OF THE FIELD.

AGNES STRICKLAND.

Fair lilies of Jerusalem,
  Ye wear the same array
As when imperial Judah's stem
  Maintained its regal sway.

By sacred Jordan's desert tide
  As bright ye blossom on
As when your simple charms outvied
  The pride of Solomon.

Ye flourished when the captive band,
  By prophets warned in vain,
Were led to far Euphrates' strand,
  From Jordan's pleasant plain,

In hostile lands to weep and dream
  Of things that still were free,
And sigh to see your golden gleam,
  Sweet flowers of Galilee!

Ye have survived Judæa's throne,
  Her temple's overthrow,
And seen proud Salem sitting lone,
  A widow in her woe.

But, lilies of Jerusalem,
  Through every change ye shine;
Your golden urns unfading gem
  The fields of Palestine.

PART II.

REVELATION: THE OLD TESTAMENT.

THE BIBLE.

BERNARD BARTON.

LAMP of our feet! whereby we trace
  Our path, when wont to stray;
Stream from the fount of heavenly grace!
  Brook by the traveller's way!

Bread of our souls! whereon we feed;
  True manna from on high!
Our guide and chart! wherein we read
  Of realms beyond the sky.

Pillar of fire, through watches dark!
  Of radiant cloud, by day!
When waves would whelm our tossing bark,
  Our anchor and our stay!

4 *

Pole-star on life's tempestuous deep!
  Beacon! when doubts surround;
Compass! by which our course we keep;
  Our deep-sea lead, to sound!

Riches in poverty! our aid
  In every needful hour!
Unshaken rock! the pilgrim's shade,
  The soldier's fortress tower!

Our shield and buckler in the fight!
  Victory's triumphant palm!
Comfort in grief! in weakness, might!
  In sickness, Gilead's balm!

Childhood's preceptor! manhood's trust!
  Old age's firm ally!
Our hope — when we go down to dust —
  Of immortality!

Pure oracles of Truth Divine!
  Unlike each fabled dream
Given forth from Delphos' mystic shrine,
  Or groves of Academe!

Word of the Ever-living God!
  Will of his glorious Son!
Without thee how could earth be trod?
  Or heaven itself be won?

Yet to unfold thy hidden worth,
  Thy mysteries to reveal,
That SPIRIT which first gave thee forth
  Thy volume must UNSEAL!

And we, if we aright would learn
  The wisdom it imparts,
Must to its heavenly teachings turn
  With simple, child-like hearts!

PLEDGES OF MERCY.

JOHN KEBLE. — CHRISTIAN YEAR.

"I do set my bow in the cloud, and it shall be for a token of a covenant between me and the earth." — Gen. ix. 13.

SWEET Dove! the softest, steadiest plume
  In all the sun-bright sky,
Brightening in ever-changeful bloom,
  As breezes change on high; —

Sweet Leaf! the pledge of peace and mirth,
  "Long sought and lately won,"
Blest increase of reviving earth,
  When first it felt the sun; —

Sweet Rainbow! pride of summer days,
High set at Heaven's command,
Though into drear and dusky haze
Thou melt on either hand ; —

Dear tokens of a pardoning God,
We hail ye, one and all,
As when our fathers walked abroad,
Freed from their twelvemonth's thrall.

How joyful from the imprisoning ark
On the green earth they spring!
Not blither, after showers, the lark
Mounts up with glistening wing.

So home-bound sailors spring to shore,
Two oceans safely past;
So happy souls, when life is o'er,
Plunge in the empyreal vast.

What wins their first and fondest gaze
In all the blissful field,
And keeps it through a thousand days?
Love, face to face revealed; —

Love, imaged in that cordial look
Our Lord in Eden bends
On souls that sin and earth forsook
In time to die his friends.

And what most welcome and serene
  Dawns on the Patriarch's eye
In all the emerging hills so green,
  In all the brightening sky?

What but the gentle rainbow's gleam,
  Soothing the wearied sight
That cannot bear the solar beam,
  With soft undazzling light?

Lord, if our fathers turned to thee
  With such adoring gaze,
Wondering frail man thy light should see
  Without thy scorching blaze, —

Where is our love, and where our hearts,
  We who have seen thy Son,
Have tried thy Spirit's winning arts,
  And yet we are not won?

The Son of God in radiance beamed
  Too bright for us to scan,
But we may face the rays that streamed
  From the mild Son of Man.

There, parted into rainbow hues,
  In sweet, harmonious strife,
We see celestial love diffuse
  Its light o'er Jesus' life.

God, by his bow, vouchsafes to write
This truth in heaven above;
As every lovely hue is light,
So every grace is love.

ANGELIC VISITANTS.

CHARLES MACKAY.

On Mamre's plain, beside the Patriarch's door
The ministering angels sat; — the world was young,
And men beheld what they behold no more.
Ah no! the harps of heaven are not unstrung!
The angelic visitants may yet appear
To those who seek them! Lo! at Virtue's side,
Its friend, its prop, its solace, and its guide,
Walks Faith, with upturned eyes and voice of cheer,
A visible angel. Lo, at Sorrow's call,
Hope hastens down, an angel fair and kind,
And whispers comfort whatsoe'er befall;
While Charity, the seraph of the mind,
White-robed and pure, becomes each good man's guest,
And makes this earth a heaven to all who love her best.

SONG OF THE MANNA-GATHERERS.

KEBLE. — LYRA INNOCENTIUM.

" This is the bread which the Lord hath given you to eat."

Comrades, haste! the tent's tall shading
Lies along the level sand
Far and faint: the stars are fading
O'er the gleaming western strand.
Airs of morning
Freshen the bleak, burning land.

Haste, or ere the third hour glowing
With its eager thirst prevail
O'er the moist pearls, now bestrowing
Thymy slope and rushy vale, —
Dews celestial,
Left when earthly dews exhale.

Ere the bright good hour be wasted,
Glean, not ravening, nor in sloth:
To your tent bring all untasted; —
To thy father, nothing loth,
Bring thy treasure:
Trust thy God, and keep thy troth.

Trust him: care not for the morrow;
Should thine omer overflow,

And some poorer seek to borrow,
  Be thy gift nor scant nor slow.
    Wouldst thou store it?
  Ope thine hand and let it go.

Trust his daily work of wonder,
  Wrought in all his people's sight:
Think on yon high place of thunder,
  Think upon the unearthly light
    Brought from Sinai,
  When the prophet's face grew bright.

Think, the glory yet is nigh thee,
  Power unfelt arrests thine arm,
Love aye watching to deny thee
  Stores abounding to thy harm.
    Rich and needy
  All are levelled by love's charm.

Sing we thus our songs of labor
  At our harvest in the wild,
For our God and for our neighbor,
  Till six times the morn have smiled,
    And our vessels
  Are with twofold treasure piled.

For that one, that heavenly morrow,
  We may care and toil to-day:
Other thrift is loss and sorrow,
  Savings are but thrown away.

Hoarded manna! —
Moths and worms shall on it prey.

While the faithless and unstable
Mars with work the season blest,
We around thy heaven-sent table
Praise thee, Lord, with all our best.
Signs prophetic
Fill our week, both toil and rest.

Comrades, what our sires have told us, —
Watch and wait, for it will come;
Smiling vale shall soon enfold us
In a new and vernal home:
Earth will feed us
From her own benignant womb.

We beside the wondrous river
In the appointed hour shall stand,
Following, as from Egypt ever,
The bright cloud and outstretched hand:
In thy shadow
We shall rest, on Abraham's land.

Not by manna-showers at morning
Shall our board be then supplied,
But a strange pale gold, adorning
Many a tufted mountain-side,
Yearly feed us,
Year by year our murmurings chide.

There, no prophet's touch awaiting,
  From each cool, deep cavern start
Rills, that since their first creating
  Ne'er have ceased to sing their part.
    Oft we hear them
  In our dreams, with thirsty heart.

O, when travel-toils are over,
  When above our tranquil nest
All our guardian angels hover,
  Will our hearts be quite at rest?
    Nay, fair Canaan
  Is not heavenly Mercy's best.

Know ye not, our glorious Leader
  Salem may but see, and die?
Israel's guide and nurse and feeder
  Israel's hope from far must eye,
    Then, departing,
  Find a worthier throne on high.

Dimly shall fond fancy trace him,
  Dim, though sweet, her dreams shall prove,
Wondering what high powers embrace him,
  Where in light he walks above,
    Where, in silence
  Sleeping, hallows heath or grove.

Deeps of blessing are before us:
  Only, while the desert sky

And the sheltering cloud hang o'er us,
  Morn by morn, obediently,
    Glean we manna,
  And the song of Moses try.

THE BURIAL OF MOSES.

DUBLIN UNIVERSITY MAGAZINE.

"And he buried him in a valley in the land of Moab, over against Bethpeor; but no man knoweth of his sepulchre unto this day." — Deut. xxxiv. 6.

By Nebo's lonely mountain,
  On this side Jordan's wave,
In a vale in the land of Moab,
  There lies a lonely grave,
And no man dug that sepulchre,
  And no man saw it e'er ;
For the angels of God upturned the sod,
  And laid the dead man there.

That was the grandest funeral
  That ever passed on earth,
But no man heard the trampling,
  Or saw that train go forth.

Noiselessly as the daylight
  Comes when the night is done,
And the crimson streak on ocean's cheek
  Grows into the great sun;

Noiselessly as the spring-time
  Her crown of verdure weaves,
And all the trees on all the hills
  Open their thousand leaves:
So, without sound of music,
  Or voice of them that wept,
Silently down, from the mountain's crown,
  The great procession swept.

Perchance the bald old eagle,
  On gray Bethpeor's height,
Out of his rocky eyrie
  Looked on the wondrous sight;
Perchance the lion stalking
  Still shuns that hallowed spot:
For beast and bird have seen and heard
  That which man knoweth not.

But when the warrior dieth,
  His comrades in the war,
With arms reversed and muffled drum,
  Follow the funeral car.
They show the banners taken,
  They tell his battles won,

And after him lead his masterless steed,
  While peals the minute gun.

Amid the noblest of the land
  Men lay the sage to rest,
And give the bard an honored place,
  With costly marble drest,
In the great minster transept,
  Where lights like glories fall,
And the sweet choir sings, and the organ rings
  Along the emblazoned wall.

This was the bravest warrior
  That ever buckled sword;
This the most gifted poet
  That ever breathed a word;
And never earth's philosopher
  Traced with his golden pen
On the deathless page truths half so sage
  As he wrote down for men.

And had he not high honor?
  The hill-side for his pall,
To lie in state while angels wait
  With stars for tapers tall,
And the dark rock pines like tossing plumes
  Over his bier to wave,
And God's own hand in that lonely land
  To lay him in the grave.

In that deep grave without a name,
  Whence his uncoffined clay
Shall break again, most wondrous thought!
  Before the Judgment Day,
And stand with glory wrapped around
  On the hills he never trod,
And speak of the strife that won our life
  With the Incarnate Son of God.

O lonely tomb in Moab's land!
  O dark Bethpeor's hill!
Speak to these curious hearts of ours,
  And teach them to be still.
God hath his mysteries of grace,
  Ways that we cannot tell;
He hides them deep, like the secret sleep
  Of him he loved so well.

RUTH.

A. A. WATTS.

Entreat me not to leave thee so,
  Or turn from following thee;
Where'er thou goest I will go,
  Thy home my home shall be!

The path thou treadest, — hear my vow, —
  By me shall still be trod;
Thy people be my people now;
  Thy God shall be my God!

Reft of all else, to thee I cleave,
  Content if thou art nigh;
Whene'er thou grievest, I will grieve,
  And where thou diest, die!

And may the Lord, whose hand hath wrought
  This weight of misery,
Afflict me so, and more, if aught
  But death part thee and me!

NAAMAN'S SERVANT.

KEBLE. — LYRA INNOCENTIUM.

"Who hath despised the day of small things?"

"Who for the like of me will care?"
  So whispers many a mournful heart,
When in the weary, languid air,
  For grief or scorn, we pine apart.

So haply mused yon little maid,
From Israel's breezy mountains borne,
No more to rest in Sabbath shade,
Watching the free and wavy corn.

A captive now, and sold and bought,
In the proud Syrian's hall she waits,
Forgotten — such her moody thought —
Even as the worm beneath the gates.

But One who ne'er forgets is here:
He hath a word for thee to speak:
O serve him yet in duteous fear,
And to thy Gentile lord be meek.

So shall the healing Name be known
By thee on many a heathen shore,
And Naaman on his chariot throne
Wait humbly by Elisha's door, —

By thee desponding lepers know
The sacred waters' sevenfold might.
Then wherefore sink in listless woe?
Christ's poor and needy! claim your right, —

Your heavenly right, to do and bear
All for his sake; nor yield one sigh
To pining doubt; nor ask, "What care
In the wide world for such as I?"

THE LIBATION.

H. WARE, JR. — "FEAST OF TABERNACLES."

HIGH-PRIEST.

'T IS done. The praise is said. Another rite
Succeeds. Bring forth the sacred golden bowl;
And let the appointed priest convey it down
To Siloa's hallowed fountain. Let him draw
The sparkling waters; and with cautious step,
In glad procession, bring them up the mount,
And bear them to the altar of the Lord.
Attend him, ye that will; and, ye that will,
Abide, till with loud trump, and echoing shout,
And waving palms, the absent throng return.

WOMEN.

They go; they pass the gates; the sacred courts
They leave; their distant tread dies on the ear.
Wait not in silence for their slow return;
But wake the echoes of the Holy Place
With song, and warble forth the coming rite.

SONG (WOMAN).

Flow on, flow on, thou bright, clear stream!
  Flow on, thou fair, perpetual fount!
Transparent as the sun's warm beam,
  Bathe the stern foot of Judah's mount.

The sun above, thy waves below,
Unsullied shines, unsullied flow;
Thou as the crystal heavens art pure,
And like the heavens thou shalt endure.

The Temple crowns Moriah's height,
  Thy waters murmur at its base;
That seems Jehovah's throne of light,
  Thou his exhaustless fount of grace.
And when the emblems we would join
Of holy Love and Power divine,
We draw thy waters from their bed,
And pour them on the mountain's head.

(*Trumpet.*)

PRIEST.

They come, they come! their signal notes resound;
Their steps approach; their gladdening songs draw near.

PEOPLE (*returning*).

Hosanna! hosanna! we bring the libation,
The waters that flow from the fount of salvation.

HIGH-PRIEST.

Now let the sacred element be borne
To the high altar's top; there, with the wine
Already hallowed for the sacrifice,

Let it be mingled. With a reverent hand
Then pour the mixture out; while, flinging high
Their verdant palms, with solemn shout and song,
The people dance around their glorious shrine.

PEOPLE.

Hosanna! hosanna! pour out the libation!
  Glory and beauty, O altar, to thee!
With gladness we draw from the wells of salvation
  Waters of life, ever flowing and free.

Joy to thee, joy to thee, life-giving river!
  Glory and beauty, O altar, to thee!
The streams of salvation roll onward for ever, —
  Life to the universe, boundless and free.

HIGH-PRIEST.

Now tell your children what this rite intends;
What mean these glowing forms, these words of joy.

PRIEST.

    The prophet gave the blow;
Forth gushed the cool, refreshing wave,
The parched and perishing to save,
    Far as its waters flow.
Recalled to life, the dying band
Pressed eager to the destined land.

So, in some latter day,
When Israel lies in woe and fear,
Her great Anointed shall appear,
To chase her dark dismay.
From Him a holier stream shall flow,
To save the world from darker woe.

O, haste the glorious hour!
Haste, David's Son, illustrious King!
Come to thy waiting saints, and bring
Thy glory, peace, and power.
Hosanna! let the people cry;
Hosanna! earth and heaven reply.

PART III.

THE GOSPEL.

A CHRISTMAS HYMN.

ALFRED DOMETT.

It was the calm and silent night!
  Seven hundred years and fifty-three
Had Rome been growing up to might,
  And now was queen of land and sea!
No sound was heard of clashing wars,
  Peace brooded o'er the hushed domain;
Apollo, Pallas, Jove, and Mars
  Held undisturbed their ancient reign,
    In the solemn midnight,
      Centuries ago!

'T was in the calm and silent night!
  The senator of haughty Rome
Impatient urged his chariot's flight,
  From lordly revel rolling home.

Triumphal arches, gleaming, swell
His breast with thoughts of boundless sway;
What recked the Roman what befell
A paltry province far away,
In the solemn midnight,
Centuries ago?

Within that province far away
Went plodding home a weary boor;
A streak of light before him lay,
Fallen through a half-shut stable-door
Across his path. He paused, for naught
Told what was going on within;
How keen the stars, his only thought;
The air how calm, and cold, and thin,
In the solemn midnight,
Centuries ago!

O strange indifference! — low and high
Drowsed over common joys and cares;
The earth was still, but knew not why;
The world was listening — unawares!
How calm a moment may precede
One that shall thrill the world for ever!
To that still moment none would heed,
Man's doom was linked, no more to sever,
In the solemn midnight,
Centuries ago!

It is the calm and solemn night!
  A thousand bells ring out, and throw
Their joyous peals abroad, and smite
  The darkness, charmed and holy now!
The night that erst no shame had worn,
  To it a happy name is given;
For in that stable lay, new-born,
  The peaceful Prince of earth and heaven,
    In the solemn midnight,
      Centuries ago!

THE CHRISTMAS BELL.

ROBERT P. ROGERS.

Long ages it hath been ringing
  Since the angels sang by night,
And the star bent over the manger
  With its benison of light.

I hear the stream of its music
  Flow down the distance past,
A lullaby breathed to the present,
  A requiem to the past.

It comes on the air of winter,
  And the air is filled with snow,
So that the sound is deadened
  Till the music is deep and low.

But every ear that will listen
  May catch its wavering tone
And every heart find a meaning
  Meant for itself alone.

To some it comes as a warning
  Of trial's turbulent tide,
That will strengthen the feeble spirit,
  Or humble its erring pride.

While to many, the young and happy
  Who have little pain to bear,
It peals like the bells of a bridal
  That play with the summer air.

And to others, the pale and weary
  Who have garnered their sheaves,
It flows with a heavenly summons,
  Like the dropping of autumn leaves.

To the wretched, the sorely tempted,
  To the bowed, subdued by sorrow,
It comes with the voice of blessing,
  And whispers hope for the morrow.

But to all of us wandering pilgrims
  O may these varied chimes
Ring as a beautiful prelude
  To another march of times,

Bringing us sweet assurance
  Of the love of earthly friends,
And the care of the dear departed,
  And the hope that heaven sends.

And so will the angel music,
  This midnight dark and deep,
As it floats around our pillows,
  Hush every care to sleep.

And our dreams of untroubled slumber,
  Like shepherds, will watch on high
The star of joy and of promise
  As it shone in Bethlehem's sky.

DANGER OF PRAISE.

KEBLE. — LYRA INNOCENTIUM.

"And he confessed and denied not; but confessed, I am not the Christ."

When mortals praise thee, hide thine eyes,
  Nor in thy Master's wrong
Take to thyself his crown and prize;
  Yet more in heart than tongue.

None holier than the Desert priest
  Beneath the Law's dim sky,
Yet in Heaven's kingdom with the least,
  We read, he might not vie.

No member, yet, of Christ the Son,
  No Gospel prophet he;
Only a voice from out the throne
  Of dread yet blest decree.

If he confessed, nor dared deny,
  Woe to that Christian's heart
Who in man's praise would walk on high,
  And steal his Saviour's part!

And ah! to him what tenfold woe,
  Who hides so well his sin,
Through earth he seems a saint to go,
  Yet dies impure within!

Pray we our Lord, one pang to send
  Of deep, remorseful fear
For every smile of partial friend;—
  Praise be our penance here!

SONNET.

SACRED OFFERING.

Matthew, Chapter iv.

Upon the mountain's height he stood, — below,
The kingdoms of the world around him spread
Their glories to his view. The Tempter said,
" Fall down and worship me; I will bestow
Upon thee all these things." " Hence! thou shalt bow
To God alone!" replied the Holy One;
" Him only shalt thou serve. — Satan, begone!"
Awed by the voice divine, and threatening brow,
The Tempter instant fled, and, borne on wing
Of love, the ministering angels come
In robes of light, and heaven's immortal bloom,
Aid from above with gentle hands to bring;
And shall we tremble on our high career,
When He who guarded Jesus still is near?

CANA.

J. F. CLARKE.

Dear Friend! whose presence in the house,
  Whose gracious word benign,
Could once, at Cana's wedding feast,
  Change water into wine, —

Come, visit us, and when dull work
  Grows weary, line on line,
Revive our souls, and make us see
  Life's water glow as wine.

Gay mirth shall deepen into joy,
  Earth's hopes shall grow divine,
When Jesus visits us, to turn
  Life's water into wine.

The social talk, the evening fire,
  The homely household shrine,
Shall glow with angel visits when
  The Lord pours out the wine.

For when self-seeking turns to love,
  Which knows not mine and thine,
The miracle again is wrought,
  And water changed to wine.

SONNET.

SACRED OFFERING.

Luke, Chapter iv.

He stood within the Temple; on his brow
  Sat heavenly wisdom, and his Father's love;
The holy book before him; and below,
  The people round their gracious Saviour move;
The page, with great Isaiah's vision fraught,
  Then with a voice divine the Master read:
"The spirit of the Lord is on me, — taught
  To preach the Gospel to the poor, and led
By Him to heal the broken heart, to preach
  Deliverance to the captives, to the blind
Restore their sight again; and I must reach
  Aid to the bruised ones, and their chains unbind."
O words of love and mercy! still shall rest
Thy spirit, Jesus, in thy follower's breast.

THE IMAGE OF THE EARTHY.

T. H. GILL.

O MEAN may seem this house of clay,
  Yet 't was the Lord's abode;
Our feet may mourn this thorny way,
  Yet here Emmanuel trod.

This fleshly robe the Lord did wear,
  This watch the Lord did keep,
These burdens sore the Lord did bear,
  These tears the Lord did weep.

This world the Master overcame,
  This death the Lord did die;
O vanquished world! O glorious shame!
  O hallowed agony!

O vale of tears, no longer sad,
  Wherein the Lord did dwell!
O holy robe of flesh, that clad
  Our own Emmanuel!

Our very frailty brings us near
  Unto the Lord of heaven;
To every grief, to every tear,
  Such glory strange is given.

SONNET.

SACRED OFFERING.

Matthew, Chapter xi.

" Come unto me," the heavenly Teacher said,
  " All ye with labor and with toil opprest,
  And I will give your wearied spirits rest;
And bear my yoke, and in my footsteps tread,
For I am meek and lowly, and will lead
  Your souls to peace; for gentle is my yoke,
  My burden light." O, not in vain were spoke,
Saviour, thy words of mercy, still decreed
To cheer my drooping soul, upon its way
  Through earthly scenes of trial, care, and strife!
  Yes, I will come to thee; thy words of life
Shall calm each anxious thought, and chase away
The hopes, the fears, the vain desires, that rise
To lure my spirit from its kindred skies.

THE SAVIOUR IN THE THRONG OF HUMAN LIFE.

BY JOHN STERLING.

Amid the gay and noisy throng
  Around me fluttering, wheeling, shining,
My ears are filled with shout and song;
  But yet my soul is still repining.

In every face around I see
  Some heart-felt curse in silence working;
Each eye reflects my sins on me,
  And shows me all within me lurking.

'Mid bounding joy and passion's glow,
  'Mid sportive bursts of mutual gladness,
Thin shades arise from far below,
  Where boils a secret gulf of madness.

A quivering cheek, a faltering glance,
  One throb, one sigh, the whole revealing;
In all the flashing, whirling dance,
  I see a world of shipwreck reeling.

And while I fain would pause and think,
  Me too the tumult onward presses;
In vain I strive, in vain I shrink;
  My breast the hour's vague fiend possesses.

'Mid wreaths and gems, 'mid masks and crowns,
  'Mid brows austere, or smooth from sorrow,
On all alike one ruin frowns,
  And bodes for all one fearful morrow.

And 't is the worst despair to know,
  By pangs within my bosom aching,
How deep in each the root of woe,
  How many a heart is slowly breaking.

But while my sad, bewildered view
  The wide confusion vainly traces,
One look I see serenely true,
  Among the false and loveless faces.

Like yon blue sky, when first it shows
  The storm-tost ship how Heaven hath pity;
Or some pure mountain breeze that blows
  Its healing o'er a plague-struck city.

A voice not loud, like wind or wave,
  A look made low by conscious greatness,
Where all is calm, and deep, and grave,
  With a full soul's mature sedateness.

By Him subdued to thought and peace,
  The crowd no more in tumult wander;
The sounds of surging riot cease,
  And hearts high swollen devoutly ponder.

By his mild glance and sober power
  Renewed to tranquil aspiration,
My soul escapes the reckless hour,
  And learns his spirit's pure elation.

To thee, O God! a man redeemed,
  With all a world to thee returning,
We own the light from Him that beamed,
  In Him the source for ever burning.

So, 'mid our stormy griefs and joys,
  May He still teach unforced devotion,
Recall our shaken being's poise,
  And clear and deepen all emotion.

SONNET.

SACRED OFFERING.

John, Chapter xi.

"I AM the resurrection and the life,—
  He who believes in me shall never die."
  These, Master, were thy words; and still rely
My hopes unmoved upon them, 'mid the strife
Of earthly care; and then I follow thee
  To the cold grave where Lazarus is laid.

I see thy tears, and Mary asks thine aid, —
The aid is present. "That thou hearedst me,
Father, I thank thee"; and thou criest aloud
To Lazarus, "Come forth!" He lives, he breathes,
The funeral garb is rent, the many wreaths
Of death are torn away, and the pale shroud;
Whilst wondering forms around the Saviour move,
And own the presence of Almighty Love.

LAZARUS AND MARY.

TENNYSON. — "IN MEMORIAM."

When Lazarus left his charnel-cave,
And home to Mary's house returned,
Was this demanded, — if he yearned
To hear her weeping by his grave?

"Where wert thou, brother, those four days?"
There lives no record of reply,
Which, telling what it is to die,
Had surely added praise to praise.

From every house the neighbors met,
The streets were filled with joyful sound;

A solemn gladness even crowned
The purple brows of Olivet.

Behold a man raised up by Christ!
The rest remaineth unrevealed;
He told it not; or something sealed
The lips of that Evangelist.

Her eyes are homes of silent prayer,
Nor other thought her mind admits
But, he was dead, and there he sits,
And he that brought him back is there.

Then one deep love doth supersede
All other, when her ardent gaze
Roves from the living brother's face,
And rests upon the Life indeed.

All subtle thought, all curious fears,
Borne down by gladness so complete,
She bows, she bathes the Saviour's feet
With costly spikenard and with tears.

Thrice blest whose lives are faithful prayers,
Whose loves in higher love endure;
What souls possess themselves so pure,
Or is there blessedness like theirs?

COMFORT.

MRS. E. B. BROWNING.

SPEAK low to me, my Saviour, low and sweet
From out the hallelujahs, sweet and low,
Lest I should fear and fall, and miss thee so
Who art not missed by any that entreat.
Speak to me as to Mary at thy feet, —
And if no precious gums my hands bestow,
Let my tears drop like amber, while I go
In reach of thy divinest voice complete
In humanest affection, — thus, in sooth,
To lose the sense of losing! As a child,
Whose song-bird seeks the wood for evermore,
Is sung to in its stead by mother's mouth, —
Till, sinking on her breast, love-reconciled,
He sleeps the faster that he wept before.

COMMUNION HYMN.

N. L. FROTHINGHAM.

"Do this in remembrance of me."
"How he was known of them in breaking of bread."

"REMEMBER me," the Saviour said,
On that forsaken night,
When from his side the nearest fled,
And death was close in sight.

Through all the following ages' track
  The world remembers yet;
With love and worship gazes back,
  And never can forget.

But who of us has seen his face,
  Or heard the words he said?
And none can now his look retrace
  In breaking of the bread.

O blest are they, who have not seen,
  And yet believe him still!
They know him, when his praise they mean,
  And when they do his will.

We hear his word along our way;
  We see his light above;
Remember when we strive and pray,
  Remember when we love.

THE MASTER.

S. D. ROBBINS.

Thou art our Master! Thou of God the Son,
    Of man the friend;
By thee alone the victory is won:
    Our souls defend!

Thou art the Master! let us love thy word:
Thy spirit give!
Let us obey thee as our risen Lord,
Obey, and live.

Thou art our Master! with thy cross, thy crown,
Thou Crucified!
Now from thy starry throne look gently down,
With us abide!

Thou art our Master! through the narrow way
Thou once didst tread,
Lead thy disciples upward to the day!
Thou living Head!

Thou art our Master! at thy feet we cast
Our burdens now.
The yoke of Love we take; O, bind us fast!
To thee we bow.

Thou art our Master! through our earthly home
No guide but thee!
And when thy kingdom unto us shall come,
Our servant be!*

* Luke xii. 37.

HYMN TO JESUS.

SYLVESTER JUDD.

O Son of God! thy children we;
Train us in holiness:
As thou the Father's image bore,
Thine own on us impress.

O Bread of God! our natures crave
The lost beatitude:
The Father gave thee meat unknown;
Give us thy flesh and blood.

O Vine of God! of thee bereft,
Our virtues wilt and die:
Thou wert the Father's tender care;
Shield us when danger 's nigh.

O Word of God! thy voice we hear,
And hail the truth divine;
To thy commandments, broad and pure,
Our hearts and ways incline.

O Love of God! we seek to dwell
In love, and God, and thee;
The end of woes, the end of sins,
Shall love's perfection be.

Light of the World! our path illume;
  The shadowy fear disperse;
Shine on these realms of woe and sin;
  Undo the heavy curse.

Water of Life! our life's sweet spring;
  In us thy stream renew;
On lowly grace thy grace distil,
  Kindly as Hermon's dew.

O Shepherd! guard thy little flock;
  Keep us from strife and guile;
Serene our life; be our life's close
  Calm as a summer isle.

O Crucified! we share thy cross;
  Thy passion too sustain;
We die thy death, to live thy life,
  And rise with thee again.

O Glorified! thy glory breaks;
  Our new-born spirits sing;
Salvation cometh with the morn;
  Hope spreads an heavenward wing.

"I WILL NOT LEAVE YOU COMFORTLESS."

MARGARET FULLER OSSOLI.

O FRIEND divine! this promise dear
Falls sweetly on the weary ear!
Often, in hours of sickening pain,
It soothes me to thy rest again.

Might I a true disciple be,
Following thy footsteps faithfully,
Then should I still the succor prove
Of Him who gave his life for love.

When this fond heart would vainly beat
For bliss that ne'er on earth we meet,
For perfect sympathy of soul
From those such heavy laws control;

When, roused from passion's ecstasy,
I see the dreams that filled it fly, —
Amid my bitter tears and sighs
Those gentle words before me rise.

With aching brows and feverish brain
The founts of intellect I drain,
And con with over-anxious thought
What poets sung and heroes wrought.

Enchanted with their deeds and lays,
I with like gems would deck my days;
No fires creative in me burn,
And, humbled, I to Thee return.

When blackest clouds around me rolled
Of scepticism drear and cold,
When love and hope and joy and pride
Forsook a spirit deeply tried,—

My reason wavered in that hour,
Prayer, too impatient, lost its power;
From thy benignity a ray
I caught, and found the perfect day.

A head revered in dust was laid;
For the first time I watched my dead;
The widow's sobs were checked in vain,
And childhood's tears poured down like rain.

In awe I gaze on that dear face,
In sorrow, years gone by retrace,
When, nearest duties most forgot,
I might have blessed, and did it not!

Ignorant, his wisdom I reproved,
Heedless, passed by what most he loved,
Knew not a life like his to prize,
Of ceaseless toil and sacrifice.

No tears can now that hushed heart move,
No cares display a daughter's love;
The fair occasion lost, no more
Can thoughts more just to thee restore

What can I do? and how atone
For all I 've done, and left undone?
Tearful I search the parting words
Which the beloved John records.

"Not comfortless!" I dry my eyes,
My duties clear before me rise; —
Before thou think'st of taste or pride,
See home-affections satisfied!

Be not with generous *thoughts* content,
But on well-doing constant bent:
When self seems dear, self-seeking fair,
Remember this sad hour in prayer!

Though all thou wishest fly thy touch,
Much can one do who loveth much.
More of thy spirit, Jesus! give,
Not comfortless, though sad, to live.

And yet not sad, if I can know
To copy Him who here below
Sought but to do his Father's will,
Though from such sweet composure still

My heart be far. Wilt thou not aid
One whose best hopes on thee are stayed?
Breathe into me thy perfect love,
And guide me to thy rest above!

COMMUNION HYMN.

N. L. FROTHINGHAM.

"And he took bread, and gave thanks."

The Son of God gave thanks,
  Before the bread he broke:
How high that calm devotion ranks
  Among the words he spoke!

Thanks, 'mid those troubled men;
  Thanks, in that dismal hour;
The world's dark prince advancing then
  In all his rage and power.

Thanks, o'er that loaf's dread sign;
  Thanks, o'er that bitter food;
And o'er the cup, that was not wine,
  But sorrow, fear, and blood.

And shall our griefs resent
  What God appoints as best,
When he, in all things innocent,
  Was yet in all distressed?

Shall we unthankful be
  For all our blessings round,
When in that press of agony
  Such room for thanks he found?

O shame us, Lord! — whate'er
  The fortunes of our days, —
If, suffering, we are weak to bear,
  If, favored, slow to praise.

HYMN.

J. PIERPONT.

"And when they had sung a hymn, they went out into the Mount of Olives." — Matthew xxvi. 30.

The winds are hushed; the peaceful moon
  Looks down on Zion's hill;
The city sleeps; 't is night's calm noon,
  And all the streets are still, —

Save when, along the shaded walks,
  We hear the watchman's call,
Or the guard's footstep, as he stalks
  In moonlight on the wall.

How soft, how holy, is this light!
  And hark! a mournful song,
As gentle as these dews of night,
  Floats on the air along.

Affection's wish, devotion's prayer,
  Are in that holy strain;
'T is resignation, not despair;
  'T is triumph, though 't is pain.

'T is Jesus and his faithful few,
  That pour that hymn of love;
O God! may we the song renew
  Around thy board above!

CHRIST IN THE GARDEN.

J. KEBLE. — CHRISTIAN YEAR.

"Saying, Father, if thou be willing, remove this cup from me; nevertheless, not my will, but thine, be done." — Luke xxii. 42.

O Lord my God, do thou thy holy will!
I will lie still, —
I will not stir, lest I forsake thine arm,
And break the charm
Which lulls me, clinging to my Father's breast,
In perfect rest.

Wild Fancy, peace! thou must not me beguile
With thy false smile:
I know thy flatteries and thy cheating ways;
Be silent, Praise,
Blind guide with siren voice, and blinding all
That hear thy call.

Come, Self-devotion, high and pure,
Thoughts that in thankfulness endure,
Though dearest hopes are faithless found,
And dearest hearts are bursting round.
Come, Resignation, spirit meek,
And let me kiss thy placid cheek,
And read, in thy pale eye serene,
Their blessing who by faith can wean

Their hearts from sense, and learn to love
God only, and the joys above.

They say, who know the life divine,
And upward gaze with eagle eyne,
That by each golden crown on high,
Rich with celestial jewelry,
Which for our Lord's redeemed is set,
There hangs a radiant coronet,
All gemmed with pure and living light,
Too dazzling for a sinner's sight,
Prepared for virgin souls, and them
Who seek the martyr's diadem.

Nor deem, who to that bliss aspire,
Must win their way through blood and fire.
The writhings of a wounded heart
Are fiercer than a foeman's dart.
Oft in Life's stillest shade reclining,
In desolation unrepining,
Without a hope on earth to find
A mirror in an answering mind,
Meek souls there are, who little deem
Their daily strife an angel's theme,
Or that the rod they take so calm
Shall prove in heaven a martyr's palm.

And there are souls that seem to dwell
Above this earth, — so rich a spell

Floats round their steps, where'er they move,
From hopes fulfilled and mutual love.
Such, if on high their thoughts are set,
Nor in the stream the source forget,
If prompt to quit the bliss they know,
Following the Lamb where'er he go,
By purest pleasures unbeguiled
To idolize or wife or child, —
Such wedded souls our God shall own
For faultless virgins round his throne.

. . . . . . The cross on Calvary
Uplifted high
Beams on the martyr host, a beacon light
In open fight.

To the still wrestlings of the lonely heart
He doth impart
The virtue of his midnight agony,
When none was nigh,
Save God and one good angel, to assuage
The tempest's rage.

Mortal! if life smile on thee, and thou find
All to thy mind,
Think, who did once from heaven to hell descend,
Thee to befriend:
So shalt thou dare forego, at his dear call,
Thy best, thine all.

"O Father! not my will, but thine, be done!"—
So spake the Son.
Be this our charm, mellowing earth's ruder noise,
Of griefs and joys;
That we may cling for ever to thy breast,
In perfect rest!

THE TWO SAYINGS.

MRS. E. B. BROWNING.

Two sayings of the Holy Scriptures beat,
Like pulses, in the Church's brow and breast;
And by them we find rest for our unrest,
And, heart-deep in salt tears, do yet entreat
God's fellowship, as if on heavenly seat.
The first is JESUS WEPT,—whereon is prest
Full many a sobbing face that drops its best
And sweetest waters on the record sweet:—
And one is where the Christ denied and scorned
LOOKED UPON PETER. Oh, to render plain,
By help of having loved a little, and mourned,
That look of sovran love and sovran pain,
Which He who could not sin, yet suffered, turned
On him who could reject, but not sustain!

THE SAVIOUR'S DYING HOUR.

MRS. HEMANS.

O Son of Man!
Shadows of earth closed round thee fearfully!
All that on us is laid,
All the deep gloom,
The desolation and the abandonment,
The dark amaze of death,
All upon Thee too fell,
Redeemer! Son of Man!

But the keen pang
Wherewith the silver cord
Of earth's affection from the soul is wrung, —
The uptearing of those tendrils which have grown
Into the quick strong heart, —
This, *this*, the passion and the agony
Of battling love and death,
Surely was not for *Thee*,
Holy One! Son of God!

Yes, my Redeemer!
E'en this cup was thine!
Fond wailing voices called thy spirit back;
E'en midst the mighty thoughts
Of that last crowning hour,
E'en on thine awful way to victory,

Wildly they called thee back!
And weeping eyes of love
Unto thy heart's deep core
Pierced through the folds of death's mysterious veil;
Sufferer! thou Son of Man!

Mother-tears were mingled
With thy costly blood-drops,
In the shadow of the atoning cross;
And the friend, the faithful,
He that on thy bosom,
Thence imbibing heavenly love, had lain,—
He, a pale sad watcher,—
Met with looks of anguish
All the anguish in *thy* last meek glance,
Dying Son of Man!

Oh! therefore unto thee,
Thou that hast known all woes
Bound in the girdle of mortality!
Thou that wilt lift the reed
Which storms have bruised,—
To thee may sorrow through each conflict cry;
And in that tempest hour when love and life
Mysteriously must part,
When tearful eyes
Are passionately bent
To drink earth's last fond meaning from our gaze,
Then, then forsake us not!

Shed on our spirits then
The faith and deep submissiveness of thine!
Thou that didst love,
Thou that didst weep and die,
Thou that didst rise, a victor glorified!
Conqueror! thou Son of God!

THE CRUCIFIXION.

F. H. HEDGE.

'T WAS the day when God's Anointed
Died for us the death appointed,
Bleeding on the dreadful cross;
Day of darkness, day of terror,
Deadly fruit of ancient error,
Nature's fall, and Eden's loss!

Haste, prepare the bitter chalice!
Gentile hate and Jewish malice
Lift the royal victim high, —
Like the serpent, wonder-gifted,
Which the Prophet once uplifted, —
For a sinful world to die!

Conscious of the deed unholy,
Nature's pulses beat more slowly,
And the sun his light denied;

Darkness wrapped the sacred city,
And the earth with fear and pity
        Trembled when the Just One died.

It is finished, Man of sorrows!
From thy cross our nature borrows
        Strength to bear and conquer thus.
While exalted there we view thee,
Mighty Sufferer, draw us to thee,
        Sufferer victorious!

Not in vain for us uplifted,
Man of sorrows, wonder-gifted!
        May that sacred symbol be.
Eminent amid the ages,
Guide of heroes and of sages,
        May it guide us still to thee!

Still to thee, whose love unbounded
Sorrow's deep for us hath sounded,
        Perfected by conflicts sore.
Glory to thy cross for ever!
Star that points our high endeavor
        Whither thou hast gone before.

"DARKNESS SHROUDED CALVARY."

SARAH F. ADAMS.

Darkness shrouded Calvary,
An earthquake rent the Temple's veil;
Human grief and human fear
Uttered mournful wail;
There came a voice like light athwart the skies,
" To-day thou 'lt be with me in Paradise."

Darkness shrouds humanity
When death doth sunder heart from heart;
Human love and human hope
Cannot bear to part:
Again that voice is heard athwart the skies,
" To-day thou 'lt be with me in Paradise."

MARY BY THE CROSS.

W. J. FOX.

Jews were wrought to cruel madness;
Christians fled in fear and sadness;
Mary stood the cross beside:

At its foot her foot she planted,
By the dreadful scene undaunted,
Till the gentle Sufferer died.

Poets oft have sung her story,
Painters decked her brow with glory,
Priests her name have deified.

But no worship, song, or glory
Touches like that simple story, —
Mary stood the cross beside.

And when, under fierce oppression,
Goodness suffers like transgression,
Christ again is crucified;

But if love be there, true-hearted,
By no grief or terror parted,
Mary stands the cross beside.

SONNET.

SACRED OFFERING.

John, Chapter xix.

STRETCHED on the cross, with mortal woe oppressed,
The Son of Man breathed forth his parting sighs;
Darkness o'erspread the earth; and then the cries
Of smitten hearts were heard, and nearer pressed

His mother, and the follower whom he loved.
"Mother, behold thy son!" the Saviour said, —
"Behold thy mother!" The o'erwhelming dread
Of death came o'er him; yet his pale lips moved
With love and mercy still, as the base crowd
Mocked at his sufferings, and the tumult grew.
"Father, forgive! they know not what they do!"
Was heard amid his anguish, and aloud
He cried, "'T is finished!" bowed his hallowed head,
And to his God the chastened spirit fled.

LOOKING UNTO JESUS.

MRS. MILES.

Thou who didst stoop below,
To drain the cup of woe,
And wear the form of frail mortality,
Thy blessed labors done,
Thy crown of victory won,
Hast passed from earth, — passed to thy home on high.

It was no path of flowers,
Through this dark world of ours,
Beloved of the Father, thou didst tread;

And shall we, in dismay,
Shrink from the narrow way,
When clouds and darkness are around it spread?

O Thou, who art our life,
Be with us through the strife;
Thy own meek head by rudest storms was bowed;
Raise thou our eyes above,
To see a Father's love
Beam, like a bow of promise, through the cloud.

E'en through the awful gloom
Which hovers o'er the tomb,
That light of love our guiding star shall be;
Our spirits shall not dread
The shadowy way to tread,
Friend, Guardian, Saviour, which doth lead to thee.

LINES WRITTEN AT THE TEMPLE OF THE HOLY SEPULCHRE.

COPIED FROM A VERY OLD EDITION OF SANDYS'S TRAVELS.

Saviour of mankind, Man! Emmanuel!
Who, sinless, died for sin; who vanquished hell;
The first-fruits of the grave; whose life did give
Light to our darkness; in whose death we live;

O, strengthen thou my faith, correct my will,
So that the latter death may not devour
My soul sealed with thy seal. So in the hour
When thou, whose body sanctified this tomb,
Unjustly judged, a glorious Judge shall come
To judge the world with justice, by that sign
I may be known, and entertained for thine.

MARY AND JOHN, BEFORE THE RESURRECTION.

S. G. BULFINCH.

My mother! in the awful hour
 When darkness o'er us lay,
While, fainting by the Blest One's cross,
 My arm became thy stay,
Did not his gentle voice then seal
 The bond for thee and me,
And give me for the coming time
 To be a son to thee?

O privilege of all most high!
 O boon of all most dear!
Still, still, in sweet, sad memory
 That voice I seem to hear.
Then come, my mother! share the cot
 Thy Jesus oft hath blest,

Far hence, where blue Gennesareth
  Expands his peaceful breast.

The boat lies idle on the strand,
  The net hangs by the wall;
In happier hour, when hope was high,
  For him I left them all.
Now, for his sake and thine, I turn
  Back to that quiet sea.
Farewell, ye proud and guilty towers!
  My mother! come with me!

There oft, when eve's advancing shades
  O'er hill and lake are thrown,
Will we recall the varied past,
  And weep for hopes now gone.
Then will we waken slumbering faith,
  And lift our brightening eyes
To Him, who e'en from this deep gloom
  Can bid the light arise.

Yes, we will trust! My thought retains
  Words of mysterious power
The Loved One spoke, as o'er his soul
  Darkened the destined hour.
That he should rise again! O joy!
  But ah! for hope too dear!
Some mystic meaning sure was there,
  That time shall render clear.

Perchance another, in his might,
  With burning words shall come,
And lead repentant Israel forth
  To mourn above his tomb.
Perchance his rising will be there
  Where we with him shall rise,
To meet the Father's smile of love
  In yonder holy skies!

But now, the night in watching spent,
  How glorious breaks the day!
The sisters hasten to the tomb,
  The last sad rites to pay;
And lo! our brethren's scattered band
  Are gathering mournfully, —
All here except that sacred form
  We never more may see!

SONNET.

SACRED OFFERING.

Matthew, Chapter xxviii.

At early morn before the Saviour's tomb
  The holy women wept. The conscious world
Shook with an earthquake, and amid the gloom
  An angel form appeared, and instant hurled

The mighty stone away. Immortal bloom
Was round about him, and as lightning shone
His eyes and polished brow. The soldiers, come
To guard the sacred sepulchre, fell down,
Like dead men to the earth, o'ercome with fear.
Then spoke the angel messenger: "I know
Ye seek the Christ; fear not, he is not here,
For he is risen, as he promised, — lo!
I 've told you, — and he goes to Galilee;
There once again the Saviour ye shall see."

THE WALK TO EMMAUS.

COWPER.

It happened on a solemn eventide,
Soon after He that was our Surety died,
Two bosom friends, each pensively inclined,
The scene of all those sorrows left behind,
Sought their own village, busied as they went
In musings worthy of the great event:
They spake of him they loved, of him whose life,
Though blameless, had incurred perpetual strife,
Whose deeds had left, in spite of hostile arts,
A deep memorial graven on their hearts.
A recollection, like a vein of ore,
The farther traced, enriched them still the more;

They thought him, and they justly thought him, one
Sent to do more than he appeared to have done,—
To exalt a people, and to place them high
Above all else,—and wondered he should die.
Ere yet they brought their journey to an end,
A stranger joined them, courteous as a friend,
And asked them, with a kind, engaging air,
What their affliction was, and begged a share.
Informed, he gathered up the broken thread,
And, truth and wisdom gracing all he said,
Explained, illustrated, and searched so well
The tender theme on which they chose to dwell,
That, reaching home, "The night," they said, "is near;
We must not now be parted,—sojourn here."
The new acquaintance soon become a guest,
And, made so welcome at their simple feast,
He blest the bread, but vanished at the word,
And left them both exclaiming, "'Twas the Lord!
Did not our hearts feel all he deigned to say?
Did they not burn within us by the way?"

THE ASCENSION.

FABER.

WHY is thy face so lit with smiles,
  Mother of Jesus, why?
And wherefore is thy beaming look
  So fixed upon the sky?

From out thine overflowing eyes
  Bright lights of gladness part,
As though some gushing fount of joy
  Had broken in thy heart.

His rising form on Olivet
  A summer's shadow cast;
The branches of the hoary trees
  Drooped as the shadow passed.

The silver cloud hath sailed away,
  The skies are blue and free;
The road that vision took is now
  Sunshine and vacancy.

The feet which thou hast kissed so oft,
  Those living feet, are gone;
Mother! thou canst but stoop and kiss
  Their print upon the stone.

Yes! he hath left thee, mother dear!
His throne is far above;
How canst thou be so full of joy
When thou hast lost thy Love?

O surely earth's poor sunshine no
To thee mere gloom appears,
When he is gone who was its light
For three and thirty years.

Why do not thy sweet hands detain
His feet upon their way?
O, why doth not the mother speak,
And bid her Son to stay?

Ah, no! thy love is rightful love,
From all self-seeking free;
The change that is such gain to him
Can be no loss to thee!

'T is sweet to feel our Saviour's love,
To feel his presence near;
Yet loyal love his glory holds
A thousand times more dear.

Ah! never is our love so pure
As when refined by pain,
Or when God's glory upon earth
Finds in our loss its gain!

THE CHRISTIAN THRONES.

W. P. LUNT.

"Then answered Peter, and said unto him, Behold, we have forsaken all, and followed thee; what shall we have therefore?

"And Jesus said unto them, Verily I say unto you, that ye which have followed me, in the regeneration, when the Son of Man shall sit on the throne of his glory, ye also shall sit upon twelve thrones, judging the twelve tribes of Israel." — Matthew xix. 27, 28.

"O NOT in vain, my chosen band,
Have ye deserted all for me;
Ye 're held by an almighty hand,
That guides the car of destiny.
The awe-struck nations, as ye go
In triumph through the earth, shall bow.

"Thrones shall be yours, — not earthly thrones,
The crumbling seats of human pride, —
The King of kings shall give you crowns,
And raise you honored to my side.
Where'er Messiah's glory spreads,
Reflected light shall grace your heads."

It was no chief in war-array,
Whose battle-share had ploughed the soil
Of many a realm, thus gave away
The harvest of his bloody toil.
These words of hope by Him were said
Who had not where to lay his head.

Though humble was his earthly state
  From whom the cheering promise came,
And mean as was their seeming fate
  Who heard announced their future fame,
The advancing ages yet beheld
The wondrous prophecy fulfilled.

Saviour! awhile to death submit;
  Let frantic foes above thee rave;
Hell and the world in vain unite,—
  Thy gate of triumph is the grave.
The worm thy fellow once, but now
Heaven's diadem adorns thy brow.

And ye who stood around the tree,
  And knew his sufferings full well,—
Ye trusted that it had been he
  Should have redeemed lost Israel.
Ye trusted! Have ye lost that trust?
The cross is borne,—the tomb is burst.

Your hopes revive; but not at once
  Must ye the promised height attain;
They who would share the recompense
  Must drink the cup of shame and pain,—
Must bear to be tormented, spurned,—
Must give their bodies to be burned!

The cup is drained; in many a land
  Your scattered limbs dishonored lie;

And mustering fast at Heaven's command,
  The ministers of vengeance fly;
The blood-stained cross they bear on high,
Blest symbol now of victory.

What shriek is that which rends the air?
  Jerusalem, with streaming eyes,
Utters imploringly her cry,
  And looks for safety to the skies.
Too late, alas! she seeks her good;
Her garments are defiled with blood.

God's holy prophets she hath slain, —
  From God's own Son she turned away;
Her corse lies mangled on the plain, —
  The eagles gather to their prey.
They flap in triumph o'er the dead;
Jerusalem! thy glory 's fled!

The Roman Cæsars rule the world;
  Jehovah's sway is given to Jove;
Another standard is unfurled, —
  The eagle cowers to the dove, —
Before the nation's wondering eyes
The Apostolic Thrones arise.

The Northern whirlwind sweeps in vain
  O'er the fair fields of Italy,
These thrones untouched by Goth remain,
  And Vandal vengeance passes by;

Christ and his holy twelve command
The homage of the barbarous band.

Europe awhile, struck with dismay,
  Saw in her sky the Crescent's light;
It faded 'midst the blaze of day,
  It only decks the brow of night.
Where science, art, and freedom shine
The Gospel mingles light divine.

To unknown shores, truth's guiding sta1
  Lights the discoverer o'er the sea;
To Western wilds it points afar,
  The future empire of the free;
And here, in freedom's chosen land,
The Christian Thrones exalted stand.

The ocean islands catch the light
  Which on their gloom in glory breaks;
And superstition, with affright,
  Through all her vast dominions quakes.
The regions that have felt her rod
Must be surrendered back to God.

It comes, — the long predicted day,
  When all mankind, with one accord,
Shall fling their idol gods away,
  And pay due homage to the Lord!
While earthly states to ruin tend,
The Christian Thrones shall know no end.

PART IV.

MEDITATION, PRAYER, AND PRAISE.

HOLY BAPTISM.

J. KEBLE. — CHRISTIAN YEAR.

Where is it mothers learn their love?
In every church a fountain springs,
O'er which the Eternal Dove
Hovers on softest wings.

What sparkles in that lucid flood
Is water by gross mortals eyed:
But seen by faith, 't is blood
Out of a dear Friend's side.

A few calm words of faith and prayer,
A few bright drops of holy dew,
Shall work a wonder there,
Earth's charmers never knew.

O happy arms, where cradled lies,
  And ready for the Lord's embrace,
    That precious sacrifice,
      The darling of his grace!

Blest eyes, that see the smiling gleam
  Upon the slumbering features glow,
    When the life-giving stream
      Touches the tender brow!

Or when the holy cross is signed,
  And the young soldier duly sworn
    With true and fearless mind
      To serve the Virgin-born.

But happiest ye, who sealed and blest
  Back to your arms your treasure take,
    With Jesus' mark impressed,
      To nurse for Jesus' sake:

To whom — as if in hallowed air
  Ye knelt before some awful shrine —
    His innocent gestures wear
      A meaning half divine:

By whom Love's daily touch is seen
  In strengthening form and freshening hue,
    In the fixed brow serene,
      The deep yet eager view.

Who taught thy pure and even breath
  To come and go with such sweet grace?
    Whence thy reposing faith,
      Though in our frail embrace?

O tender gem, and full of heaven!
  Not in the twilight stars on high,
    Not in moist flowers at even,
      See we our God so nigh.

Sweet one, make haste and know Him too,
  Thine own adopting Father love,
    That like thine earliest dew
      Thy dying sweets may prove.

BABY CARL.

MRS. S. F. CLAPP.

Out from clouds of fear and darkness,
Clothed in sunbeams, thou didst fall,
Filling all the house with brightness
        At thy coming,
        Baby Carl!
Light mysterious lingers with thee,
From beyond the prison wall
That our hands of clay have builded

Round thy spirit,
Baby Carl!

When thou smilest, art thou hearing
Some mysterious angel call?
Or do bright celestial visions
Float about thee,
Baby Carl?
By thy beauty and thy sweetness
Thou dost hold all hearts in thrall;
Willing hands obey the mandates
Of imperious
Baby Carl.

Underneath thy folded eyelids
Creep no phantoms to appall;
Smile-wreathed dreams betray no glimpses
Of life's battle,
Baby Carl.
Time shall bear the conflict to thee;
Late or soon, it comes to all;
Veiled a while in love paternal
From thy vision,
Baby Carl!

Clouds of care shall close about thee,
Fear shall make thy heart to quail;
Powerless is our love to shield thee
From the combat,
Baby Carl.

Ere thy innocence forsakes thee,
Or the angel-watches fail,
May the Father's love recall thee
Back to heaven,
Baby Carl!

WEST'S PICTURE OF THE INFANT SAMUEL.

EPHRAIM PEABODY.

In childhood's spring, — ah, blessed spring! —
(As flowers closed up at even
Unfold in morning's earliest beam,)
The heart unfolds to Heaven.
Ah, blessed child! that trustingly
Adores, and loves, and fears,
And to a Father's voice replies,
Speak, Lord! thy servant hears.

When youth shall come, — ah, blessed youth!
If still the pure heart glows,
And in the world and word of God
Its Maker's language knows;
If in the night and in the day,
'Midst youthful joys or fears,
The trusting heart can answer still,
Speak, Lord! thy servant hears.

When age shall come, — ah, blessed age!
  If in its lengthening shade,
When life grows faint, and earthly lights
  Recede, and sink, and fade, —
Ah, blessed age! if then heaven's light
  Dawns on the closing eye,
And faith unto the call of God
  Can answer, Here am I!

TO MY GUARDIAN ANGEL.

(FOR CHILDREN.)

FABER.

Dear angel! ever at my side,
  How loving must thou be,
To leave thy home in heaven to guard
  A little child like me!

Thy beautiful and shining face
  I see not, though so near;
The sweetness of thy soft, low voice
  I am too deaf to hear.

I cannot feel thee touch my hand
  With pressure light and mild,

To check me, as my mother did
  When I was but a child.

But I have felt thee in my thoughts
  Fighting with sin for me;
And when my heart loves God, perhaps
  The sweetness is from thee.

And when, dear spirit, I kneel down
  Morning and night to prayer,
Something there is within my heart
  Which tells me thou art there.

And thou in life's last hour wilt bring
  A fresh supply of grace,
And afterwards wilt let me kiss
  Thy beautiful, bright face.

LINES TO D. G. T. OF SHERWOOD.

MRS. M. G. HORSFORD.

Blessings on thee, noble boy!
  With thy sunny eyes of blue,
Speaking in their cloudless depths
  Of a spirit pure and true.

In thy thoughtful look and calm,
 In thy forehead broad and high,
We have seemed to meet again
 One whose home is in the sky.

Thou to earth art still a stranger,
 To life's tumult and unrest;
Angel-visitants alone
 Stir the fountains in thy breast.

Thou hast yet no Past to shadow
 With a fear thy Future's light,
And the present spreads before thee
 Boundless as the infinite.

But each passing hour must waken
 Energies that slumber now,
Manhood with its fire and action
 Stamp that fair, unfurrowed brow.

Into life's sublime arena,
 Opening through the world's broad mart,
Bear thy mother's gentle spirit,
 And her kind and loving heart.

With exalted hope and purpose,
 To the great and good aspire;
Downward, in unsullied glory
 Hand the honor of thy sire.

With that love for truth and justice
  After annals shall declare
Highest proof of moral greatness,
  Nobly live and nobly dare.

Cloudless pass thine infant days;
  Childhood bring thee naught but joy;
Manhood, thought and dignity:
  Blessings on thee, noble boy!

WRITTEN IN A PRAYER-BOOK GIVEN TO MY DAUGHTER.

BERNARD BARTON.

My creed requires no form of prayer;
  Yet would I not condemn
Those who adopt with pious care
  Their use as aids to them.

One God hath fashioned them and me;
  One Spirit is our guide;
For each, alike, upon the tree
  One common Saviour died!

Each the same trumpet-call shall wake,
  To face one judgment-seat;
God give us grace, for Jesus' sake,
  In the same heaven to meet!

THE SOUL.

R. C. WATERSTON.

WHY was this ponderous planet hung in air,
With grandeur robed, and crowned with beauty
fair?
Hear ye the voice which whispers from afar,
Speaks in each breeze, is echoed from each star!
For Man the myriad wheels of Nature roll;
He is the central sun, the Living Soul.

View the glad earth, — her oceans and her rills,
Her verdant valleys and her vine-clad hills;
Behold with rapture all that meets thy sight,
Beaming with love, and touched with heavenly
light;
But know that earth's magnificence combined,
Shrinks to a point, when balanced with the MIND!

Let thy free thought go forth, and nobly dare
To pierce high heaven, and view each splendor
there,
Draw the bright curtain from creation's face,
And, trembling, gaze through boundless fields of
space;
Yet feel that those vast scenes before thee brought
Are not so wondrous as thy Power of Thought!

O Thou, who "spake creation into birth,"
Then formed the Soul as sovereign of the earth,
Naught is so vast in thy majestic plan,
As thine own image symbolized in man!
Teach us to know, and humbly to revere
The mighty marvels thou hast centred here;
To bow with awe before each inward light,
The sense of wrong, the consciousness of right.
The aspirations which to heaven would soar, —
The power to love, contemplate, and adore;
Mysterious thought, which with an eagle glance
Measures the depth of infinite expanse;
Immortal hope, that may for ever shine; —
These live within, and burn with power divine!

Arouse thee, Soul! and turn thy piercing eye
On thine own inward being! Learn the high
And holy purposes for which on earth
Jehovah gave thy wondrous spirit birth:
Ponder each heavenly hope, each earthly strife,
And know the long — forever — of thy life!

Up! child of earth, and, wondering, behold
This world of thought. Let all its powers unfold
Before thine awe-struck vision. Guard with care
The faintest spark which God has kindled there;
Let no untimely frost, nor blight of sin,
Blast the immortal life which buds within!

THE BUILDING OF THE HOUSE.

CHARLES MACKAY.

I HAVE a wondrous house to build,
  A dwelling, humble yet divine;
A lowly cottage to be filled
  With all the jewels of the mine.
How shall I build it strong and fair, —
This noble house, this lodging rare,
  So small and modest, yet so great?
How shall I fill its chambers bare
With use, with ornaments, with state?

My God hath given the stone and clay;
  'T is I must fashion them aright;
'T is I must mould them day by day,
  And make my labor my delight;
This cot, this palace, this fair home,
This pleasure-house, this holy dome,
  Must be in all proportions fit,
That heavenly messengers may come
  To lodge with him who tenants it.

No fairy bower this house must be,
  To totter at each gale that starts,
But of substantial masonry,
  Symmetrical in all its parts:

Fit in its strength to stand sublime,
For seventy years of mortal time,
  Defiant of the storm and rain,
And well attempered to the clime
  In every cranny, nook, and pane.

I 'll build it so, that if the blast
  Around it whistle loud and long,
The tempest when its rage has passed
  Shall leave its rafters doubly strong.
I 'll build it so that travellers by
Shall view it with admiring eye,
  For its commodiousness and grace:
Firm on the ground, — straight to the sky, —
  A meek, but goodly dwelling-place.

Thus noble in its outward form,
  Within I 'll build it clean and white;
Not cheerless cold, but happy warm,
  And ever open to the light.
No tortuous passages or stair,
No chamber foul, or dungeon lair,
  No gloomy attic, shall there be,
But wide apartments, ordered fair,
  And redolent of purity.

With three compartments furnished well,
  The house shall be a home complete;
Wherein, should circumstance rebel,
  The humble tenant may retreat.

The first, a room wherein to deal
With men for human nature's weal,
  A room where he may work or play,
And all his social life reveal
  In its pure texture, day by day.

The second, for his wisdom sought,
  Where, with his chosen book or friend,
He may employ his active thought
  To virtuous or exalted end.
A chamber lofty and serene,
With a door-window to the green,
  Smooth-shaven sward, and arching bowers,
Where lore, or talk, or song between
  May gild his intellectual hours.

The third an oratory dim,
  But beautiful, where he may raise,
Unheard of men, his daily hymn
  Of love and gratitude and praise;
Where he may revel in the light
Of things unseen and infinite,
  And learn how little he may be,
And yet how awful in thy sight,
  Ineffable Eternity!

Such is the house that I must build;
  This is the cottage, this the dome,
And this the palace, treasure-filled,
For an immortal's earthly home.

O noble work of toil and care!
O task most difficult and rare!
  O simple but most arduous plan!
To raise a dwelling-place so fair,
  The sanctuary of a Man.

NEW YEAR'S DAY.

W. B. O. PEABODY.

How fast the rushing files of years
  Move on their stern array!
The messenger of joy and tears,
  Of rising or decay.
While many a weary heart grows cold
To see how soon the tale is told,
The *young* heart wakes,—the young eye seems
To catch new brightness from the gleams
Of glorious and reviving beams
  That crown the New Year's day.

This day reminds us of the past,
  When young existence ran,
A radiant current, bright and fast,
  Before the storms began,
And threw the shadow of their wrath
Across the brightness of our path,

To cloud the visions, sweet and strange,
Of youthful fancy in its range,
And teach us what a dreary change
    It is — to be a man.

Bright as the good old winter blaze
    The high remembrance burns,
Soon as one glimpse of early days
    The weary soul discerns.
The rising of the New Year's sun
Brings back those pleasures, one by one;
The early "wish," — the glad reply
Of little voices ringing high,
Before the dawn was in the sky, —
    The very sound returns.

Then, all that day, the sparkle played
    In every youthful eye;
The stern old teacher kindly laid
    His week-day terrors by.
The New Year's wish was warmly given;
There was no chill but that of heaven,
To check the free and joyous glow
Of young emotions in their flow!
And even the wild winds moaned low
    Through all the frozen sky.

And when, around the sounding blaze,
    The evening circle spread,

The firelight cast on every face
    Its deep and radiant red ;
We talked of darkness and its powers,
Of ghosts that walked in shivering towers, —
Till, listening to the tales of wonder,
Each sound was like the startling thunder,
And our young hearts were rent asunder,
    In that delighted dread.

Like one who from a distant land
    Returns, his home to see,
And starts, to see the stranger stand
    Beneath his father's tree,
To us the coming New Year's day
Tells but of pleasure far away;
The *day*, without the *joy*, returns;
The *fire*, but not the *bosom*, burns;
And there the spirit sadly learns
    What man was meant to be.

The dial hands of heaven sublime
    Wheel round their brilliant way,
And point to man the lapse of time,
    While man grows old and gray.
His joys and sorrows, hopes and fears,
Are sinking in the grave of years;
But this dark prospect is not all;
And though the shades of evening fall,
He yet *may* hear a *heavenly* call
    To hail a New Year's day.

ON NEW YEAR'S DAY.

SACRED OFFERING.

Light of another year again I see,
  And its first day is mine! But whether I
  May see it join the past eternity,
My Father and my God! depends on thee.
O grant its hours, as on swift wing they flee,
  In peace and goodness, compassed by thy love,
  May swiftly glide; so shall my soul not move,
Though sorrow waits the dark futurity.
Thus would I consecrate this year; and oh!
  If other prayer is beating in my breast,
  It is for those I love, that they may rest
In the same trust, the same high comfort know;
That when our years their destined race have run,
We each may find the meed of virtue won.

CLOSE OF THE YEAR.

EBENEZER ELLIOTT.

Another year is swallowed by the sea
    Of sumless waves!
Another year, thou past Eternity!
    Hath rolled o'er new-made graves.

They open yet — to bid the living weep,
Where tears are vain;
While they, unswept into the ruthless deep,
Storm-tried and sad, remain.

Why are we spared? Surely to wear away,
By useful deeds,
Vile traces, left beneath the upbraiding spray,
Of empty shells and weeds.

But there are things which time devoureth not:
Thoughts, whose green youth
Flowers o'er the ashes of the unforgot;
And words, whose fruit is truth.

Are ye not imaged in the eternal sea,
Things of to-day?
Deeds which are harvest for eternity,
Ye cannot pass away!

CHURCHES IN BOSTON.

O. W. HOLMES.

"What is thy creed?" a hundred lips inquire;
"Thou seekest God beneath what Christian spire?"
Nor ask they idly, for uncounted lies
Float upward on the smoke of sacrifice:

When man's first incense rose above the plain,
Of earth's two altars, one was built by Cain!

Uncursed by doubt, our earliest creed we take;
We love the precepts for the teacher's sake;
The simple lessons which the nursery taught
Fell soft and stainless on the buds of thought,
And the full blossom owes its fairest hue
To those sweet tear-drops of affection's dew.

Too oft the light that led our earlier hours
Fades with the perfume of our cradle flowers;
The clear, cold question chills to frozen doubt;
Tired of beliefs, we dread to live without;
O then, if Reason waver at thy side,
Let humbler Memory be thy gentle guide;
Go to thy birthplace, and, if faith was there,
Repeat thy father's creed, thy mother's prayer!

Faith loves to lean on Time's destroying arm,
And age, like distance, lends a double charm;
In dim cathedrals, dark with vaulted gloom,
What holy awe invests the saintly tomb!
There pride will bow, and anxious care expand,
And creeping avarice come with open hand;
The gay can weep, the impious can adore,
From morn's first glimmerings on the chancel floor
Till dying sunset sheds his crimson stains
Through the faint halos of the irised panes.

Yet there are graves, whose rudely-shapen sod
Bears the fresh footprints where the sexton trod,
Graves where the verdure has not dared to shoot,
Where the chance wild-flower has not fixed its root,
Whose slumbering tenants, dead without a name,
The eternal record shall at length proclaim
Pure as the holiest in the long array
Of hooded, mitred, or tiaraed clay.

. . . . .

The air is hushed; the street is holy ground;
Hark! The sweet bells renew their welcome sound;
As, one by one, awakes each silent tongue,
It tells the turret whence its voice is flung.

The Chapel,* last of sublunary things
That shocks our echoes with the name of King's,
Whose bell, just glistening from the font and forge,
Rolled its proud requiem for the second George,
Solemn and swelling, as of old it rang,
Flings to the wind its deep, sonorous clang; —
The simpler pile,† that, mindful of the hour
When Howe's artillery shook its half-built tower,
Wears on its bosom, as a bride might do,
The iron breastpin which the "Rebels" threw,
Wakes the sharp echoes with the quivering thrill
Of keen vibrations, tremulous and shrill; —

---

* King's Chapel. † The Church in Brattle Square.

Aloft, suspended in the morning's fire,
Crash the vast cymbals from the Southern
spire; * —
The Giant, † standing by the elm-clad green,
His white lance lifted o'er the silent scene,
Whirling in air his brazen goblet round,
Swings from its brim the swollen floods of sound;—
While, sad with memories of the olden time,
The Northern Minstrel ‡ pours her tender chime,
Faint, single tones, that spell their ancient song,
But tears still follow as they breathe along.

Child of the soil, whom fortune sends to range
Where man and nature, faith and customs, change,
Borne in thy memory, each remembered tone
Mourns on the winds that sigh in every zone.
When Ceylon sweeps thee with her perfumed
breeze
Through the warm billows of the Indian seas;
When—ship and shadow blended both in one—
Flames o'er thy mast the equatorial sun,
From sparkling midnight to refulgent noon
Thy canvas swelling with the still monsoon;
When through thy shrouds the wild tornado sings,
And thy poor sea-bird folds her tattered wings,
Oft will delusion o'er thy senses steal,
And airy echoes ring the Sabbath peal!

---

* The Old South Church. † Park Street Church. ‡ Christ Church.

Then, dim with grateful tears, in long array
Rise the fair town, the island-studded bay,
Home, with its smiling board, its cheering fire,
The half-choked welcome of the expecting sire,
The mother's kiss, and, still if aught remain,
Our whispering hearts shall aid the silent strain.

Ah, let the dreamer o'er the taffrail lean,
To muse unheeded, and to weep unseen;
Fear not the tropic's dews, the evening's chills,
His heart lies warm among his triple hills!

LOVE, HOPE, AND FAITH.

SYLVESTER JUDD.

Bless, holy Love! our calm retreat;
The lily 's fair, the rose is sweet;
Than rose or lily, purer bloom
The hearts thy grace and power illume.

O Hope divine! support our souls;
The shadows fall, the thunder rolls;
When terror all the land enshrouds,
With thy blue eye disperse the clouds.

The mountain hides us from the East;
In us be living Faith increased;
The mountain from its place we fling,
Or o'er its top our vision wing.

BISHOP HUBERT.

BERNARD BARTON.

'T IS the hour of even now,
And with meditative brow,
Seeking truths as yet unknown,
Bishop Hubert walks alone.

Fain would he, with earnest thought,
Nature's secret laws be taught;
Learn the destinies of man,
And creation's wonders scan.

And further yet, from these would trace
Hidden mysteries of grace,
Dive into the deepest theme,
Solve redemption's glorious scheme.

Far he has not roamed, before,
On the solitary shore,
He hast found a little child,
By its seeming play beguiled.

In the drifted, barren sand
It has scooped, with baby hand,
Small recess, in which might float
Sportive fairy's tiny boat.

From a hollow shell, the while,
See, 't is filling, with a smile,
Pool as shallow as may be
With the waters of the sea.

Hear the smiling Bishop ask,
" What can mean such infant task?"
Mark that infant's answer plain, —
" 'T is to hold yon mighty main."

" Foolish infant," Hubert cries,
" Open, if thou canst, thine eyes:
Can a hollow scooped by thee
Hope to hold the boundless sea?"

Soon that child, on ocean's brim,
Opes its eyes and turns to him:
Well does Hubert read its look,
Glance of innocent rebuke:

While a voice is heard to say,
" If the pool, thus scooped in play,
Cannot hold the mighty sea,
What must thy researches be?

"Canst thou hope to make thine own
Secrets known to God alone?
Can thy faculty confined
Compass the Eternal Mind?"

Bishop Hubert turns away,—
He has learnt enough to-day.

THE KINGDOM OF GOD.

R. C. TRENCH.

I SAY to thee, do thou repeat
To the first man thou mayest meet
In lane, highway, or open street,—

That he, and we, and all men, move
Under a canopy of love,
As broad as the blue sky above:

That doubt and trouble, fear and pain
And anguish, all are shadows vain;
That death itself shall not remain:

That weary deserts we may tread,
A dreary labyrinth may thread,
Through dark ways under ground be led:

Yet, if we will one Guide obey,
The dreariest path, the darkest way,
Shall issue out in heavenly day :

And we, on divers shores now cast,
Shall meet, our perilous voyage past,
All in our Father's house at last.

And ere thou leave him, say thou this,
Yet one word more : they only miss
The winning of that final bliss,

Who will not count it true that Love,
Blessing, not cursing, rules above,
And that in it we live and move.

And one thing further make him know, —
That to believe these things are so,
This firm faith never to forego,

Despite of all which seems at strife
With blessing, all with curses rife, —
That this *is* blessing, this *is* life.

HYMN.

CHARLES H. A. DALL.

" As for truth, it endureth and is always strong; it liveth and conquereth for evermore." — 1 Esdras iv. 38.

GREAT is the earth, O God!
But mightier still is truth;
As thou endurest, so it stands
Strong in eternal youth.

High is the pure, blue heaven;
Truth is as pure and high;
All angels bless thy righteousness,
All men repeat the cry.

Unerring flies the sun,
But truth is surer yet;
The nations, quickened in its course
Shall live, ere truth is set.

Transient are human works,
Wicked is human thought:
We perish in unrighteousness
If truth inspire us not.

Christ yesterday, to-day,
For ever, — conquers, lives;

Christ is thy truth and power for aye,
'T is Christ thy kingdom gives.

No truth but is in him,
He claims no greatness else;
The majesty of ages, he
Comes in the truth he tells.

EXAGGERATION.

MRS. BROWNING.

We overstate the ills of life, and take
Imagination,—given us to bring down
The choirs of singing angels overshone
By God's clear glory,—down our earth to rake
The dismal snows instead; flake following flake,
To cover all the corn. We walk upon
The shadow of hills across a level thrown,
And pant like climbers. Near the alder-brake
We sigh so loud, the nightingale within
Refuses to sing loud, as else she would.
O brothers! let us leave the shame and sin
Of taking vainly, in a plaintive mood,
The holy name of Grief! holy herein,
That by the grief of One came all our good.

THE STRAIGHT ROAD.

DISCIPLES' HYMN-BOOK.

Beauty may be the path to highest good,
And some successfully have it pursued.
Thou, who wouldst follow, be well warned to see
That way prove not a curvéd road to thee.
The straightest path perhaps which may be sought
Lies through the great highway men call I ought.

GLORY TO GOD ALONE.

MADAME GUYON.

O Loved! but not enough, though dearer far
Than self and its most loved enjoyments are;
None duly loves thee, but who, nobly free
From sensual objects, finds his all in thee.

Glory of God! thou stranger here below,
Whom man nor knows, nor feels a wish to know;
Our faith and reason are both shocked to find
Man in the post of honor, thee behind.

My soul, rest happy in thy low estate,
Nor hope nor wish to be esteemed or great;
To take the impression of a Will Divine,
Be that thy glory, and those riches thine.

Confess him righteous in his just decrees,
Love what he loves, and let his pleasures please;
Die daily; from the touch of sin recede;
Then thou hast crowned him, and he reigns
indeed.

A MEDITATION.

N. L. FROTHINGHAM.

Too far from thee, O Lord.
The world is close upon each captured sense;
The heart's dear idols never vanish hence;
Life's care and labor still are pressing nigh;
Its fates and passions hard about me lie; —
But Thou art dim behind thine infinite sky,
O distantly adored!

O Lord, too far from thee!
Unwingéd Time stands ever in my sight,
Flooding the Past and Now with gloom and light;
Silent, but busy, constant at my side,
It shreds away strength, beauty, joy, and pride.
Eternal! why am I from Thee so wide,
Nor thy near Presence see?

Ne'er languished for as now,
Now that the hold of Earth feels poor and frail;
Now that the cheek of Hope looks thin and pale,

And forms of buried love rise ghostly round,
And dark thoughts struggle on o'er broken ground;
Where is thy face, O Father! radiant found
With mercy on thy brow?

I know that not from far,
Not from abroad, this presence is revealed,—
To our will denied, and from our wit concealed,
No search can find Thee, no entreaty bring,—
Reason a weak, Desert a spotted thing.
O Spirit, lift me on thy dove-like wing
To realms that last and ARE!

THE OCEAN.

C. P. CRANCH.

"In a season of calm weather,
Though inland far we be,
Our souls have sight of that immortal sea
That brought us hither;
Can in a moment travel thither,
And see the children sport upon the shore,
And hear the mighty waters rolling evermore."
WORDSWORTH.

TELL me, brother, what are we?
Spirits bathing in the sea
Of Deity!
Half afloat, and half on land,
Wishing much to leave the strand,

Standing, gazing with devotion,
Yet afraid to trust the ocean, —
Such are we.

Wanting love and holiness
To enjoy the waves' caress;
Wanting faith and heavenly hope,
Buoyantly to bear us up;
Yet impatient in our dwelling,
When we hear the ocean swelling,
And in every wave that rolls
We behold the happy souls
Peacefully, triumphantly,
Swimming on the smiling sea,
Then we linger round the shore,
Lovers of the earth no more.

Once — 't was in our infancy —
We were drifted by this sea
To the coast of human birth,
To this body and this earth;
Gentle were the hands that bore
Our young spirits to the shore;
Gentle lips that bade us look
Outward from our cradle-nook
To the spirit-bearing ocean
With such wonder and devotion,
As, each stilly Sabbath day,
We were led a little way,

Where we saw the waters swell
Far away from inland dell,
And received with grave delight
Symbols of the Infinite:—
Then our home was near the sea;
"Heaven was round our infancy";—
Night and day we heard the waves
Murmuring by us to their caves,—
Floated in unconscious life,
With no later doubts at strife,
Trustful of the Upholding Power,
Who sustained us hour by hour.

Now we 've wandered from the shore,
Dwellers by the sea no more;
Yet at times there comes a tone
Telling of the visions flown,
Sounding from the distant sea
Where we left our purity:
Distant glimpses of the surge
Lure us down to ocean's verge;
There we stand, with vague distress,
Yearning for the measureless,
By half-wakened instincts driven,
Half loving earth, half loving heaven,
Fearing to put off and swim,
Yet impelled to turn to Him,
In whose life we live and move,
And whose very name is Love.

Grant me courage, Holy One,
To become indeed thy son,
And in thee, thou Parent Sea,
Live and love eternally.

SONNET.

R. C. TRENCH.

Lord, what a change within us one short hour
Spent in thy presence will prevail to make, —
What heavy burdens from our bosoms take,
What parchéd grounds refresh, as with a shower!
We kneel, and all around us seems to lower;
We rise, and all, the distant and the near,
Stands forth in sunny outline, brave and clear;
We kneel how weak, we rise how full of power!
Why, therefore, should we do ourselves this wrong,
Or others, that we are not always strong, —
That we are ever overborne with care, —
That we should ever weak or heartless be,
Anxious or troubled, when with us in prayer,
And joy, and strength, and courage, are with thee?

NEARER TO THEE.

SARAH F. ADAMS.

Nearer, my God, to thee, —
Nearer to thee!
E'en though it be a cross
That raiseth me:
Still all my song would be,
Nearer, my God, to thee, —
Nearer to thee!

Though like the wanderer,
The sun gone down,
Darkness be over me,
My rest a stone;
Yet in my dreams I'd be
Nearer, my God, to thee, —
Nearer to thee!

There let the way appear, —
Steps unto heaven;
All that thou sendest me,
In mercy given:
Angels to beckon me
Nearer, my God, to thee, —
Nearer to thee!

Then with my waking thoughts
Bright with thy praise,
Out of my stony griefs
BETHEL I'll raise;
So by my woes to be
Nearer, my God, to thee,—
Nearer to thee!

Or if on joyful wing
Cleaving the sky,
Sun, moon, and stars forgot,
Upwards I fly;
Still all my song shall be,
Nearer, my God, to thee,—
Nearer to thee!

DESIRES FOR GOD'S PRESENCE.

JONES VERY.

WILT thou not visit me?
The plant beside me feels thy gentle dew;
Each blade of grass I see
From thy deep earth its quickening moisture drew.

Wilt thou not visit me?
Thy morning calls on me with cheering tone;

And every hill and tree
Lend but one voice, the voice of thee alone.

Come! for I need thy love,
More than the flower the dew, or grass the rain;
Come, like thy holy dove,
And let me in thy sight rejoice to live again.

Yes; thou wilt visit me;
Nor plant nor tree thy eye delights so well,
As when, from sin set free,
Man's spirit comes with thine in peace to dwell.

GOD KNOWN BY LOVING HIM.

MADAME GUYON.

'T IS not the skill of human art
Which gives me power my God to know;
The sacred lessons of the heart
Come not from instruments below.

Love is my teacher. He can tell
The wonders that he learnt above;
No other master knows so well; —
'T is Love alone can tell of LOVE.

O, then of God if thou wouldst learn,
  His wisdom, goodness, glory see,
All human arts and knowledge spurn,
  Let love alone thy teacher be.

Love is my master. When it breaks,
  The morning light, with rising ray,
To thee, O God! my spirit wakes,
  And love instructs it all the day.

And when the gleams of day retire,
  And midnight spreads its dark control,
Love's secret whispers still inspire
  Their holy lessons in the soul.

MATINS.

MRS. H. B. STOWE.

STILL, still with Thee, when purple morning breaketh,
  When the bird waketh, and the shadows flee;
Fairer than morning, lovelier than the daylight,
  Dawns the sweet consciousness, I am with Thee!

Alone with Thee, amid the mystic shadows,
  The solemn hush of nature newly born;

Alone with Thee, in breathless adoration,
In the calm dew and freshness of the morn.

As in the dawning, o'er the waveless ocean,
The image of the morning-star doth rest,
So in this stillness Thou beholdest only
Thine image in the waters of my breast.

When sinks the soul, subdued by toil, to slumber,
Its closing eye looks up to Thee in prayer,
Sweet the repose beneath thy wings o'ershading,
But sweeter still to wake and find Thee there.

So shall it be at last in that bright morning
When the soul waketh, and life's shadows flee;
O in that hour, fairer than daylight dawning,
Shall rise the glorious thought, I am with Thee!

GOD THE FOUNTAIN OF LOVE TO HIS CHILDREN.

MADAME GUYON.

I LOVE my God, but with no love of mine,
For I have none to give:
I love thee, Lord; but all the love is thine,
For by thy life I live.
I am as nothing, and rejoice to be
Emptied, and lost, and swallowed up in Thee.

Thou, Lord, alone, art all thy children need,
And there is none beside;
From thee the streams of blessedness proceed;
In thee the blest abide;
Fountain of life, and all-abounding grace,
Our source, our centre, and our dwelling-place.

"DARK THE FAITH OF DAYS OF YORE."

ALTERED FROM COLERIDGE.

FOX'S COLLECTION.

Dark the faith of days of yore,
" And at evening evermore
Did the chanters, sad and saintly,
Yellow tapers burning faintly,
Doleful masses chant to thee,
Miserere, Domine!"

Bright the faith of coming days;
And when dawn the kindling rays
Of heaven's golden lamp ascending,
Happy hearts, and voices blending,
Joyful anthems chant to thee,
Te laudamus, Domine!

Night's sad "cadence dies away
On the yellow, moonlit sea;
The boatmen rest their oars, and say,
Miserere, Domine!"

Morn's glad chorus swells alway
On the azure, sunlit sea;
The boatmen ply their oars, and say,
Te laudamus, Domine!

HYMN OF THE CITY.

W. C. BRYANT.

Not in the solitude
Alone, may man commune with Heaven, or see
Only in savage wood,
Or sunny vale, the present Deity;
Or only hear his voice
Where the winds whisper and the waves rejoice.

Even here do I behold
Thy steps, Almighty! — here, amidst the crowd
Through the great city rolled,
With everlasting murmur, deep and loud,
Choking the ways that wind
'Mongst the proud piles, the work of human kind.

Thy golden sunshine comes
From the round heaven, and on their dwelling lies,
And lights their inner homes;
For them thou fill'st with air the unbounded skies,
And givest them the stores
Of ocean, and the harvests of its shores.

Thy spirit is around,
Quickening the restless mass that sweeps along;
And this eternal sound, —
Voices and footfalls of the numberless throng, —
Like the resounding sea,
Or like the rainy tempest, speaks of thee.

And when the hours of rest
Come, like a calm upon the mid-sea brine,
Hushing its billowy breast,
The quiet of that moment, too, is thine;
It breathes of Him who keeps
The vast and helpless city while it sleeps.

PART V.

ACTIVE DUTY.

ON FOR EVER.

MRS. L. J. HALL.

WINDS of the sky! ye hurry by
    On your strong and busy wings,
And your might is great, and your song is high,
    And true is the tale it sings.
    " On, on, for ever and aye!
    Round the whole earth lieth our way:
    On, on, for we may not stay!"

Murmuring stream! like a soft dream
    Goest thou stealing along,
Pausing not in the shade or gleam,
    And this is thy ceaseless song:
    " On, on, for ever and aye!
    Down to the deep lieth my way:
    On, for I may not stay!"

Queen of yon high and dim blue vault,
    Gliding past many a star,
'Mid their bright orbs thou dost not halt,
    And a voice comes down from thy car:
    " On, on, for ever and aye!
    Round the whole earth lieth my way:
    On, for I may not stay!"

Thoughts of my mind, ye hurry on;
    Whence ye come I may not know,
But from my soul ye straight are gone,
    In a ceaseless, ceaseless flow.
    " On, on, for ever and aye!
    By a behest we must obey,
    On, for we may not stay!"

Man may not stay! there is no rest
    On earth for the good man's foot;
He should go forth on errands blest,
    And toil for unearthly fruit.
    On, on, for ever and aye!
    Idle not precious hours away:
    On, for ye may not stay!

Sit ye not down in sloth's dark bower,
    Where shades o'er the spirit fall;
Pause not to wreathe the sunny flower
    That is worn in pleasure's hall.

On, on, for ever and aye!
Duties spring up along your way:
Do good, — for ye may not stay!

BEAUTY AND DUTY.

THE DIAL.

I SLEPT, — and dreamed that life was beauty;
I woke, — and found that life was duty.
Was my dream, then, a shadowy lie?
Toil on, sad heart, courageously;
And thou shalt find thy dream shall be
A noonday light and truth to thee.

PROGRESS.

T. H. GILL.

EVERLASTING! changing never!
  Of one strength, no more, no less,
Thine almightiness for ever, —
  All the same thy holiness:
      Thee eternal,
  Thee all-glorious, we possess!

But we weak ones, but we sinners,
  Would not in our poorness stay;
We, the low ones, would be winners
  Of what holy height we may,
      Ever nearer
  To thy pure and perfect day.

Shall things withered, fashions olden,
  Keep us from life's flowing spring?
Waits for us the promise golden, —
  Waits each new diviner thing?
      Onward! onward!
  Why this faithless tarrying?

By the old aspirants glorious,
  By the hearts that hopéd all,
By the strivers, half-victorious,
  By each soul heroical,
      By thy dearest,
  By thy Milton and thy Paul, —

By their holy, high achieving,
  By their visions more divine,
By each gift of our receiving
  From these mighty ones of thine,
      By the radiance
  That on us from them doth shine,

By each saving word unspoken,
  By thy truth, as yet half won,

By each idol still unbroken,
  By thy will, yet poorly done, —
    Hear us! hear us!
  Our Almighty, help us on!

Nearer to thee would we venture,
  Of thy truth more largely take,
Upon life diviner enter,
  Into day more glorious break;
    To the ages
  Fair bequests and costly make.

Ours must be a nobler story
  Than was ever writ before:
After-comers! dim our glory;
  Be your smiles and winnings more!
    Everlasting!
  Fuller grace incessant pour!

TRUE REST.

J. S. DWIGHT.

Sweet is the pleasure
  Itself cannot spoil!
Is not true leisure
  One with true toil?

Thou who wouldst taste it,
  Still do thy best;
Use it, not waste it,
  Else 't is no rest.

Wouldst behold beauty
  Near thee, — all round?
Only hath duty
  Such a sight found.

Rest is not quitting
  The busy career;
Rest is the fitting
  Of self to its sphere.

'T is the brook's motion,
  Clear without strife,
Fleeing to ocean
  After its life.

Deeper devotion
  Nowhere hath knelt;
Fuller emotion
  Heart never felt.

'T is loving and serving
  The Highest and Best!
'T is ONWARDS! unswerving;
  And that is true rest.

AROUSE THEE, SOUL!

ROBERT NICOLL.

Arouse thee, soul!
Be, what thou surely art,
An emanation from the Deity, —
A flutter of that heart
Which fills all nature, sea, and earth and sky:
Arouse thee, soul!

Arouse thee, soul!
And let the body do
Some worthy deed for human happiness,
To join, when life is through,
Unto thy name, that angels both may bless:
Arouse thee, soul!

Arouse thee, soul!
Leave nothings of the earth;
And if the body be not strong to dare,
To blessed thoughts give birth,
High as yon heaven, pure as heaven's air:
Arouse thee, soul!

THE HOURS.

JONES VERY.

THE minutes have their trusts as they go by,
To bear His love who wings their viewless flight;
To Him they bear their record as they fly,
And never from their ceaseless round alight.
Rich with the life Thou liv'st they come to me:
O may I all that life to others show,
That they from strife may rise and rest in Thee,
And all thy peace in Christ by me may know!
Then shall the morning call me from my rest,
With joyful hope that I thy child may live;
And when the evening comes 't will make me blest,
To know that Thou wilt peaceful slumbers give,
Such as Thou dost to weary laborers send,
Whose sleep from Thee doth with the dews descend.

THE FAITHFUL MONK.

LINES SUGGESTED BY AN ALLUSION IN THE MEMOIR OF REV. O. W. B. PEABODY.

CHARLES T. BROOKS.

Golden gleams of noonday fell
On the pavement of the cell,
And the monk still lingered there
In the ecstasy of prayer:
Fuller floods of glory streamed
Through the window, and it seemed
Like an answering glow of love,
From the countenance above.

On the silence of the cell
Break the faint tones of a bell.
'T is the hour when at the gate
Crowds of poor and hungry wait,
Wan and wistful, to be fed
With the friar of mercy's bread.

Hark! that chime of heaven's far bells!
On the monk's rapt ear it swells.
No! fond, flattering dream, away!
Mercy calls; no longer stay!
Whom thou yearnest here to find.
In the musings of thy mind,

God and Jesus, lo, they wait
Knocking at thy convent gate!

From his knees the monk arose;
With full heart and hand he goes,
At his gate the poor relieves,
Gives a blessing, and receives;
To his cell returned, and there
Found the angel of his prayer,
Who with radiant features said,
"Hadst thou stayed, I must have fled."

"NOT TO MYSELF ALONE."

SARGENT'S SELECTION.

"NOT to myself alone,"
The little opening flower transported cries, —
"Not to myself alone I bud and bloom;
With fragrant breath the breezes I perfume,
And gladden all things with my rainbow dyes.
The bee comes sipping, every eventide,
His dainty fill;
The butterfly within my cup doth hide
From threatening ill."

" Not to myself alone,"
The *circling* star with honest pride doth boast, —
" Not to myself alone, I rise and set;
I write upon night's coronal of jet
His power and skill who formed our myriad host;
A friendly beacon at heaven's open gate,
I gem the sky,
That man might ne'er forget, in every fate,
His home on high."

" Not to myself alone,"
The heavy-laden bee doth murmuring hum, —
" Not to myself alone, from flower to flower,
I rove the wood, the garden, and the bower,
And to the hive at evening weary come:
For man, for man, the luscious food I pile,
With busy care,
Content if I repay my ceaseless toil
With scanty share."

" Not to myself alone,"
The soaring bird with lusty pinion sings, —
" Not to myself alone I raise my song;
I cheer the drooping with my warbling tongue,
And bear the mourner on my viewless wings;
I bid the hymnless churl my anthem learn,
And God adore;
I call the worldling from his dross to turn,
And sing and soar."

"Not to myself alone,"
The streamlet whispers on its pebbly way, —
"Not to myself alone I sparkling glide;
I scatter health and life on every side,
And strew the fields with herb and floweret gay.
I sing unto the common, bleak and bare,
My gladsome tune;
I sweeten and refresh the languid air
In droughty June."

"Not to myself alone"; —
O man! forget not thou — earth's honored priest,
Its tongue, its soul, its life, its pulse, its heart —
In earth's great chorus to sustain thy part!
Chiefest of guests at love's ungrudging feast,
Play not the niggard; spurn thy native clod,
And *self* disown;
Live to thy neighbor; live unto thy God;
Not to thyself alone!

FAITH'S ANSWER.

CAROLINE WHITMARSH.

STILL, as of old, thy precious word
Is by the nations dimly heard;
The hearts its holiness hath stirred
Are weak and few.
Wise men the secret dare not tell;
Still in thy temple slumbers well
Good Eli: O, like Samuel,
Lord, here am I!

Few years, no wisdom, no renown,
Only my life can I lay down;
Only my heart, Lord! to thy throne
I bring; and pray,
That child of thine I may go forth,
And spread glad tidings through the earth,
And teach sad hearts to know thy worth.
Lord, here am I!

Thy messenger, all-loving One!
The errands of thy truth to run,
The wisdom of thy holy Son
To teach and live!
No purse or scrip, no staff or sword;—
Be pure intent my wings, O Lord!

Be innocence my magic word.
    Lord, here am I!

Young lips may teach the wise, Christ said;
Weak feet sad wanderers home have led;
Small hands have cheered the sick one's bed
    With freshest flowers:
Yet teach me, Father! heed their sighs,
While many a soul in darkness lies,
And waits thy message; make me wise!
    Lord, here am I!

And make me strong; that staff and stay,
And guide and guardian of the way,
To thee-ward I may bear, each day,
    Some precious soul.
"Speak; for I hear!" make "pure in heart,"
Thy face to see. Thy truth impart
In hut and hall, in church and mart.
    Lord, here am I!

I ask no heaven till earth be thine,
Nor glory-crown while work of mine
Remaineth here: when Earth shall shine
    Among the stars,
Her sins wiped out, her captives free,
Her voice a music unto thee,
For crown, new work give thou to me!
    Lord, here am I!

EARTH'S ANGELS.

ANONYMOUS.

WHY come not spirits from the realms of glory,
To visit earth as in the days of old, —
The times of sacred writ and ancient story?
Is heaven more distant? or has earth grown cold?

Oft have I gazed, when sunset clouds, receding,
Waved like rich banners of a host gone by,
To catch the gleam of some white pinion speeding
Along the confines of the glowing sky.

And oft, when midnight stars in distant chillness
Were calmly burning, listened late and long;
But nature's pulse beat on in solemn stillness,
Bearing no echo of the seraphs' song.

To Bethlehem's air was their last anthem given,
When other stars before the One grew dim?
Was their last presence known in Peter's prison,
Or where exulting martyrs raised their hymn?

And are they all within the veil departed?
There gleams no wing along the empyrean now;
And many a tear from human eyes has started,
Since angel touch has calmed a mortal's brow.

No: earth has angels, though their forms are moulded
But of such clay as fashions all below;
Though harps are wanting, and bright pinions folded,
We know them by the love-light on their brow.

I have seen angels by the sick one's pillow, —
Theirs was the soft tone and the soundless tread;
Where smitten hearts were drooping like the willow,
They stood "between the weeping and the dead."

And if my sight, by earthly dimness hindered,
Beheld no hovering cherubim in air,
I doubted not, for spirits know their kindred,
They smiled upon the wingless watchers there.

There have been angels in the gloomy prison, —
In crowded halls, — by the lone widow's hearth;
And where they passed, the fallen have uprisen,
The giddy paused, the mourner's hope had birth.

I have seen one, whose eloquence commanding
Roused the rich echoes of the human breast,

The blandishments of wealth and ease withstanding
That hope might reach the suffering and oppressed.

And by his side there moved a form of beauty,
Strewing sweet flowers along his path of life,
And looking up with meek and love-lent duty;
I called her angel, but he called her wife.

O, many a spirit walks the world unheeded,
That, when its veil of sadness is laid down,
Shall soar aloft with pinions unimpeded,
And wear its glory like a starry crown!

"IT PROFITETH THEE NOTHING."

DISCIPLES' HYMN-BOOK.

"My child, cleanse thou thy heart; this daily life
Of alms and works, how can it profit thee,
Except low down upon the altar burn
The hidden fire of holy charity?

"Leave here thy deeds,—go seek the inner shrine;
There watch, and wait, and pray, and tend thy soul,

Till comes the grace which gives no outward sign,
  Till heaven and earth are bound to its control!"

Father, well know I, I have utmost need
  To tend that hidden fire both night and day;
But who will warm my cold, my hungry feed,
  While I retire to weep, and watch, and pray?

Father, before the inmost, stillest shrine
  I hear the echo of that piercing cry,
And can no more implore the grace divine,
  But turn to serve this poor humanity.

Father, it may be that my light is small;
  But I had rather bear the pains that may
In purgatory my lost soul befall,
  Than leave these ones to faint upon their way.

"My child, I fear me much thou dost postpone
  God's great eternity to thy low time;
But he doth deal with every heart alone,
  And will not judge thy error like thy crime."

"BEG FROM A BEGGAR."

"*Deark d'on dearka.*" — Irish Proverb.

R. M. MILNES.

THERE is a thought so purely blest
That to its use I oft repair,
When evil breaks my spirit's rest,
And pleasure is but varied care, —
A thought to gild the stormiest skies,
To deck with flowers the bleakest moor, —
A thought whose home is paradise, —
The charities of Poor to Poor.

It were not for the rich to blame,
If they, whom Fortune seems to scorn,
Should vent their ill-content and shame
On others less or more forlorn;
But that the veriest needs of life
Should be dispensed with freer hand
Than all their stores and treasures rife,
Is not for *them* to understand.

To give the stranger's children bread,
Of your precarious board the spoil, —
To watch your helpless neighbor's bed,
And, sleepless, meet the morrow's toil; —
The gifts, not proffered once alone,
The daily sacrifice of years, —

And, when all else to give is gone,
The precious gifts of love and tears;—

What record of triumphant deed,
What virtue pompously unfurled,
Can *thus* refute the gloomy creed
That parts from God our living world?
O Misanthrope! deny who would,—
O Moralists! deny who can,—
Seeds of almost impossible good,
Deep in the deepest life of Man.

Therefore, lament not, honest soul!
That Providence holds back from thee
The means thou might'st so well control,—
Those luxuries of charity.
Manhood is nobler, as thou art;
And, should some chance thy coffers fill,
How art thou sure to keep thine heart,
To hold unchanged thy loving will?

Wealth, like all other power, is blind,
And bears a poison in its core,
To taint the best, if feeble, mind,
And madden that debased before.
It is the battle, not the prize,
That fills the hero's breast with joy;
And industry the bliss supplies,
Which mere possession might destroy.

FROM "THE MEN OF OLD."

J. G. WHITTIER.

Well speed thy mission, bold Iconoclast!
Yet all unworthy of its trust thou art,
If with dry eye, and cold, unloving heart,
Thou tread'st the solemn Pantheon of the Past,
By the great Future's dazzling hope made blind
To all the beauty, power, and truth behind.
Not without reverent awe shouldst thou put by
The cypress branches and the amaranth blooms,
Where, with clasped hands of prayer, upon their tombs
The effigies of old confessors lie,
God's witnesses, — the voices of his will,
Heard in the slow march of the centuries still!
Such were the men at whose rebuking frown,
Dark with God's wrath, the tyrant's knee went down;
Such from the terrors of the guilty drew
The vassal's freedom and the poor man's due.
St. Anselm (may he rest for evermore
In Heaven's sweet peace!) forbade, of old, the sale
Of men as slaves, and from the sacred pale
Hurled the Northumbrian buyers of the poor.
To ransom souls from bonds and evil fate,
St. Ambrose melted down the sacred plate, —

Image of saint, the chalice and the pix,
Crosses of gold, and silver candlesticks.
"MAN IS WORTH MORE THAN TEMPLES!" he replied
To such as came his holy work to chide.
And brave Cesarius, stripping altars bare,
  And coining from the Abbey's golden hoard
The captive's freedom, answered to the prayer
  Or threat of those whose fierce zeal for the Lord
Stifled their love of man, — "An earthen dish
  The last sad supper of the Master bore:
Most miserable sinners! do ye wish
  More than your Lord, and grudge his dying poor
What your own pride, and not his need, requires?
  Souls than these shining gauds he values more;
Mercy, not sacrifice, his heart desires!"

ALMSGIVING.

(AN EXTRACT.)

R. M. MILNES.

WHEN Poverty, with mien of shame,
The sense of Pity seeks to touch, —
Or, bolder, makes the simple claim
That I have nothing, you have much, —

Believe not either man or book
That bids you close the opening hand,
And with reproving speech or look
Your first and free intent withstand.

It may be that the tale you hear
Of pressing wants and losses borne
Is heaped or colored for your ear,
And tatters for the purpose worn;
But surely Poverty has not
A sadder need than this, — to wear
A mask still meaner than her lot,
Compassion's scanty food to share.

It may be that you err to give
What will but tempt to further spoil
Those who in low content would live
On theft of others' time and toil;
Yet sickness *may* have broke or bent
The active frame or vigorous will, —
Or hard occasion may prevent
Their exercise of humble skill.

It may be that the suppliant's life
Has lain on many an evil way
Of foul delight and brutal strife,
And lawless deeds that shun the day;
But how can any gauge of yours
The depth of that temptation try?

What man resists, what man endures,
Is open to one only eye.

Why not believe the homely letter,
That all you give will God restore?
The poor man *may* deserve it better,
And surely, surely wants it more:
Let but the rich man do his part,
And whatsoe'er the issue be
To those who ask, *his* answering heart
Will gain and grow in sympathy.

FROM "THE GOLDEN LEGEND."

H. W. LONGFELLOW.

THE CHAPEL. — *Vespers; after which the monks retire, a chorister leading an old monk who is blind.*

PRINCE HENRY.

THEY are all gone, save one who lingers,
Absorbed in deep and silent prayer.
As if his heart could find no rest,
At times he beats his heaving breast
With clenched and convulsive fingers,
Then lifts them trembling in the air.

A chorister, with golden hair,
Guides hitherward his heavy pace.
Can it be so? Or does my sight
Deceive me in the uncertain light?
Ah no! I recognize that face,
Though Time has touched it in his flight,
And changed the auburn hair to white.
It is Count Hugo of the Rhine,
The deadliest foe of all our race,
And hateful unto me and mine!

THE BLIND MONK.

Who is it that doth stand so near
His whispered words I almost hear?

PRINCE HENRY.

I am Prince Henry of Hoheneck,
And you, Count Hugo of the Rhine!
I know you, and I see the scar,
The brand upon your forehead, shine
And redden like a baleful star!

THE BLIND MONK.

Count Hugo once, but now the wreck
Of what I was. O Hoheneck!
The passionate will, the pride, the wrath,
That bore me headlong on my path,
Stumbled and staggered into fear,
And failed me in my mad career,
As a tired steed some evil-doer,

Alone upon a desolate moor,
Bewildered, lost, deserted, blind,
And hearing loud and close behind
The o'ertaking steps of his pursuer.
Then suddenly from the dark there came
A voice that called me by my name,
And said to me, "Kneel down and pray!"
And so my terror passed away,
Passed utterly away for ever.
Contrition, penitence, remorse,
Came on me with o'erwhelming force;
A hope, a longing, an endeavor,
By days of penance and nights of prayer,
To frustrate and defeat despair!
Calm, deep, and still is now my heart,
With tranquil waters overflowed;
A lake whose unseen fountains start,
Where once the hot volcano glowed.
And you, O Prince of Hoheneck!
Have known me in that earlier time,
A man of violence and crime,
Whose passions brooked no curb nor check.
Behold me now, in gentler mood,
One of this holy brotherhood.
Give me your hand; here let me kneel;
Make your reproaches sharp as steel;
Spurn me, and smite me on each cheek;
No violence can harm the meek,
There is no wound Christ cannot heal!

Yes; lift your princely hand, and take
Revenge, if 't is revenge you seek;
Then pardon me, for Jesus' sake!

PRINCE HENRY.

Arise, Count Hugo! let there be
No farther strife nor enmity
Between us twain; we both have erred!
Too rash in act, too wroth in word,
From the beginning we have stood
In fierce, defiant attitude,
Each thoughtless of the other's right,
And each reliant on his might.
But now our souls are more subdued;
The hand of God, and not in vain,
Has touched us with the fire of pain.
Let us kneel down, and side by side
Pray, till our souls are purified,
And pardon will not be denied!

They kneel.

THE SECRET OF PIETY.

W. R. ALGER'S "POETRY OF THE EAST."

A PINING sceptic towards a raptured saint in-
clined,
And asked him how the Boundless Lover, God,
to find.
A smile divine across the saint's pale features
stole,
And thus in wise and pitying love he poured his
soul:
"Ah, hapless wanderer! long from life's true
bliss shut out,
In night of sin forlorn and wilderness of doubt,
Prepared am I with thy sad lot to sympathize,
For o'er my own dim tracks thy dark experience
lies.
Now list and ponder deep, the secret while I tell
Of all the love with which angelic bosoms swell.
Whoso would careless tread one worm that crawls
the sod,
That cruel man is darkly alienate from God;
But he that lives, embracing all that is, in love,
To dwell with him God bursts all bounds, below,
above."

FROM "THE VISION OF SIR LAUNFAL."

J. R. LOWELL.

Sir Launfal turned from his own hard gate,
For another heir in his earldom sate:
An old, bent man, worn out and frail,
He came back from seeking the Holy Grail;*
Little he recked of his earldom's loss,
No more on his surcoat was blazoned the cross,
But deep in his soul the sign he wore,
The badge of the suffering and the poor.

Sir Launfal's raiment thin and spare
Was idle mail 'gainst the barbed air,
For it was just at the Christmas time:
So he mused, as he sat, of a sunnier clime,
And sought for a shelter from cold and snow
In the light and warmth of long ago;
He sees the snake-like caravan crawl
O'er the edge of the desert, black and small,
Then nearer and nearer, till, one by one,
He can count the camels in the sun,
As over the red-hot sands they pass
To where, in its slender necklace of grass,
The little spring laughed and leaped in the shade

* The vessel used by the Saviour at the Last Supper.

And with its own self like an infant played,
And waved its signal of palms.

"For Christ's sweet sake, I beg an alms"; —
The happy camels may reach the spring,
But Sir Launfal sees naught save the grewsome
thing,
The leper, lank as the rain-blanched bone,
That cowered beside him, a thing as lone
And white as the ice-isles of Northern seas
In the desolate horror of his disease.

And Sir Launfal said: "I behold in thee
An image of Him who died on the tree;
Thou also hast had thy crown of thorns, —
Thou also hast had the world's buffets and
scorns, —
And to thy life were not denied
The wounds in the hands and feet and side:
Mild Mary's Son, acknowledge me;
Behold, through him, I give to thee!"

Then the soul of the leper stood up in his eyes
And looked at Sir Launfal, and straightway he
Remembered in what a haughtier guise
He had flung an alms to leprosie,
When he caged his young life up in gilded mail,
And set forth in search of the Holy Grail.
The heart within him was ashes and dust;

He parted in twain his single crust,
He broke the ice on the streamlet's brink,
And gave the leper to eat and drink;
'T was a mouldy crust of coarse brown bread,
'T was water out of a wooden bowl, —
Yet with fine wheaten bread was the leper fed,
And 't was red wine he drank with his thirsty soul.

As Sir Launfal mused with a downcast face,
A light shone round about the place;
The leper no longer crouched at his side,
But stood before him glorified,
Shining and tall and fair and straight
As the pillar that stood by the Beautiful Gate, —
Himself the Gate whereby men can
Enter the temple of God in Man.

His words were shed softer than leaves from the pine,
And they fell on Sir Launfal as snows on the brine,
Which mingle their softness and quiet in one
With the shaggy unrest they float down upon;
And the voice that was calmer than silence said:
"Lo, it is I, be not afraid!
In many climes, without avail,
Thou hast spent thy life for the Holy Grail;
Behold, it is here, — this cup which thou

Didst fill at the streamlet for me but now;
This crust is my body broken for thee,
This water His blood that died on the tree;
The Holy Supper is kept indeed,
In whatso we share with another's need,—
Not that which we give, but what we share,
For the gift without the giver is bare;
Who bestows himself with his alms feeds three,—
Himself, his hungering neighbor, and me."

A PRAYER OF AFFECTION

MRS. HEMANS.

Blessings, O Father, shower!
Father of mercies! round his precious head!
On his lone walks, and on his thoughtful hour,
And the pure visions of his midnight bed,
Blessings be shed!

Father! I pray thee not
For earthly treasure to that most beloved,
Fame, fortune, power;— O, be his spirit proved
By these, or by their absence, at thy will!
But let thy peace be wedded to his lot,
Guarding his inner life from touch of ill,
With its dove-pinion still!

Let such a sense of Thee,
Thy watching presence, thy sustaining love,
His bosom guest inalienably be,
That, wheresoe'er he move,
A heavenly light serene
Upon his heart and mien
May sit undimmed! a gladness rest, his own,
Unspeakable, and to the world unknown!
Such as from childhood's morning land of dreams
Remembered faintly gleams,
Faintly remembered, and too swiftly flown!

So let him walk with Thee,
Made by thy spirit free;
And when thou call'st him from his mortal place,
To his last hour be still that sweetness given,
That joyful trust! and brightly let him part,
With lamp clear burning, and unlingering heart,
Mature to meet in heaven
His Saviour's face!

"HE FOR GOD ONLY, SHE FOR GOD IN HIM."

MRS. CAROLINE GILMAN.

When Pleasure gilds thy passing hours,
And Hope enwreathes her fairy flowers,
And Love appears with playful hand
To steal from Time his falling sand,
O, then I 'll smile with thee.

When nature's beauties bless thy sight,
And yield a thrill of soft delight,
When morning glories greet thy gaze,
Or evening twilight still delays,
Then I 'll admire with thee.

When the far-clustering stars unroll
Their bannered lights from pole to pole,
Or when the moon glides queenly by,
Looking in silence on thine eye,
I 'll gaze on heaven with thee.

When Music with her unsought lay
Awakes the household holiday,
Or Sabbath notes in concert strong
Lift up the secret wings of song,
I 'll sing those strains with thee.

But should Misfortune, hovering nigh,
Wrest from thy aching heart the sigh,
Or, with an aspect chill and drear,
Despondence draw the unbidden tear,
O, then I 'll weep with thee.

Should Poverty with withering hand
Wave o'er thy head his care-wrought wand,
And ope within thy soul the void
That haunts a mind with hope destroyed,
I 'll share that pang with thee.

When youth and youthful pleasures fly,
And earth is fading on thine eye,
When life has lost its early charm,
And all thy wish is holy calm,
I 'll love that calm with thee.

And when unerring death, at last,
Comes rushing on time's fatal blast,
And naught (not e'en my love) can save
Thy form from the encroaching grave,
I 'll share that grave with thee.

And when thy spirit soars above,
Wrapt in the foldings of God's love,
Is it too much to ask of Heaven,
That some low seat may there be given,
Where I can bow near thee?

THE YOUNG TEACHERS.

J. WEISS.

THE world throws wide its brazen gates;
  With thee we enter in;
O grant us, in our humble sphere,
  To free that world from sin!

We have one mind in Christ our Lord
  To stand and point above;
To hurl rebuke at social wrong;
  But all, O God, in love.

The star is resting in the sky;
  To worship Christ we came;
The moments haste; O touch our tongues
  With thy celestial flame!

The truest worship is a life;
  All dreaming we resign;
We lay our offerings at thy feet,—
  Our lives, O Christ, are thine!

LINES WRITTEN ON LEAVING CHARLESTON FOR THE SEASON.

1820.

SAMUEL GILMAN.

Farewell, awhile, thou hospitable spot!
  Farewell, my own adopted dwelling-place!
Scene of my future consecrated lot,
  And destined circuit of my earthly race.

Farewell, ye friends, who hung so long and true,
  With sleepless care, around my fevered bed,
And ye from whom a stranger's title drew
  Profuse attentions, delicately shed.

Yet why a stranger? since no other home
  Remains for me; e'en now, depressed, I fly
For the last time through youthful haunts to roam,
  And snatch the breezes of my native sky.

Yes, dear New England! help me from thy breast
  To wean these childish yearnings ere we part;
Help me these cords to snap, these ties to wrest,
  So wound, and stamped, and woven in my heart.

A few more bounds along thy rocky shore,
  A few more pensive walks among thy streams,

A few more greetings from dear friends of yore,
  A few more dreams, and then — no more of
    dreams.

Come, sacred, solid duty! at thy call
  My cheerful will submissively shall flow,
So thou, great Source of strength and light to all,
  Lead me the awful way my feet must go.

Teach me to bear the Christian herald's part,
  To set the slaves of sin and error free,
To guide each doubting, soothe each aching heart,
  And draw a listening, willing flock to Thee!

THE WAN REAPERS.

MRS. EMILY C. JUDSON.

I came from a land where a beautiful light
  Is slow creeping o'er hill-top and vale,
Where broad is the field, and the harvest is white,
  But the reapers are haggard and pale.

All wasted and worn with their wearisome toil,
  Still they pause not, that brave little band,
Though soon their low pillows must be the strange
    soil
  Of that distant and grave-dotted strand.

For dangers uncounted are clustering there,
The pestilence stalks uncontrolled,
Strange poisons are borne on the soft, languid air,
And lurk in each leaf's fragrant fold.

There the rose never blooms on fair woman's wan cheek,
But there 's beautiful light in her eye,
And the smile that she wears is so loving and meek,
None can doubt it came down from the sky.

There the strong man is bowed in his youth's golden prime,
But he cheerily sings at his toil,
For he thinks of his sheaves, and the garnering time
Of the glorious Lord of the soil.

And ever they turn, that brave, wan little band,
A long, wistful gaze on the West:
"Do they come, do they come from that dear distant land, —
That land of the lovely and blest?

"Do they come? Do they come? Oh! we 're feeble and wan,
And we 're passing like shadows away;
But the harvest is white, and lo! yonder the dawn!
For laborers, — for laborers, we pray!"

HENRY MARTYN AT SHIRAZ.

HENRY ALFORD.

A VISION of the bright Shiraz, of Persian bards the theme:
The vine with bunches laden hangs o'er the crystal stream,
The nightingale all day her notes in rosy thickets trills,
And the brooding heat-mist faintly lies along the distant hills.

About the plain are scattered wide, in many a crumbling heap,
The fanes of other days, and tombs where Iran's poets sleep.
And in the midst, like burnished gems in noonday light, repose
The minarets of bright Shiraz, the city of the rose.

One group beside the river bank in rapt discourse are seen,
Where hangs the golden orange on its boughs of purest green;
Their words are sweet and low, and their looks are lit with joy;
Some holy blessing seems to rest on them and their employ.

The pale-faced Frank among them sits; what brought him from afar?
Nor bears he bales of merchandise, nor teaches skill in war;
One pearl alone he brings with him, — the Book of life and death;
One warfare only teaches he, — to fight the fight of faith.

And Iran's sons are round him; and one with solemn tone
Tells how the Lord of glory was rejected by his own,
Tells, from the wondrous Gospel, of the trial and the doom,
The words divine of love and might, the scourge, the cross, the tomb.

Far sweeter to the stranger's ear those Eastern accents sound
Than music of the nightingale, that fills the air around;
Lovelier than balmiest odors sent from gardens of the rose,
The fragrance from the contrite soul and chastened lip that flows.

The nightingales have ceased to sing, the rose's leaves are shed,
The Frank's pale face in Tocat's field hath mouldered with the dead;

Alone and all unfriended, 'midst his Master's work
he fell,
With none to bathe his fevered brow, with none
his tale to tell.

But still those sweet and solemn tones about him
sound in bliss;
And fragrance from those flowers of God for ever-
more is his;
For his the meed, by grace, of those who, rich in
zeal and love,
Turn many unto righteousness, and shine as stars
above.

PART VI.

PENITENCE.

DE PROFUNDIS CLAMAVI.

C. G. FENNER.

UP from the deeps, O God, I cry to thee!
Hear the soul's prayer, hear thou her litany,
O thou who say'st, "Come, wanderer, home to
me!"

Up from the deeps of sorrow, wherein lie
Dark secrets veiled from earth's unpitying eye,
My prayers, like star-crowned angels, God-ward
fly.

Up from the deeps of joy, deep tides that swell
With fulness that the heart can never tell,
Thanks shall ring clear as rings a festal bell.

From the calm bosom when in quiet hour
God's holy spirit reigns with largest power,
Then shall each thought in prayer's white blossom flower.

From the dark mine, where slow Thought's diamond burns,
Where the Gold-spirits vein their rugged urns,
From that grim Cyclop-forge my spirit turns,

And gazes upward at thy clear blue sky,
And 'midst the light that floods it does espy
Bright stars unseen by superficial eye.

Where Sin's Red Dragons lie in caverns deep,
And glare with stony eyes that never sleep,
And o'er the Heavenly Fruit strict ward do keep;

Thence my poor heart, long struggling to get free,
Torn by the strife, in painful agony
Crieth, O God, my God, deliver me!

Up from the thickest tumult of the game,
Where spring Life's arrows with unerring aim,
My shaft of prayer, Acestes' like, shall flame.

Not from life's shallows, where the waters sleep,
A dull low marsh, where stagnant vapors creep,
But ocean-voiced, deep calling unto deep,

As he of old, King David, called to thee,
As cries the heart of poor Humanity,
"Clamavi, Domine, exaudi me!"

A LITANY.

MATTHEW ARNOLD.

Thou, who dost dwell alone, —
Thou, who dost know thine own, —
Thou, to whom all are known
From the cradle to the grave, —
Save, O save!
From the world's temptations;
From tribulations;
From that fierce anguish
Wherein we languish;
From that torpor deep
Wherein we lie asleep,
Heavy as death, cold as the grave,
Save, O save!

When the Soul, growing clearer,
Sees God no nearer;
When the Soul, mounting higher,
To God comes no nigher;

But the arch-fiend Pride
Mounts at her side,
Foiling her high emprise,
Sealing her eagle eyes,
And, when she fain would soar,
Makes idols to adore;
Changing the pure emotion
Of her high devotion
To a skin-deep sense
Of her own eloquence;
Strong to deceive, strong to enslave, —
Save, O save!

From the ingrained fashion
Of this earthly nature
That mars thy creature,
From grief that is but passion,
From mirth that is but feigning,
From tears that bring no healing,
From wild and weak complaining,
Thine own strength revealing,
Save! O save!

From doubt where all is double,
Where wise men are not strong,
Where comfort turns to trouble,
Where just men suffer wrong,
Where sorrow treads on joy,
Where sweet things soonest cloy,

Where faiths are built on dust,
Where love is half mistrust,
Hungry, and barren, and sharp as the sea,
O set us free!

O let the false dream fly
Where our sick souls do lie
Tossing continually.
O where thy voice doth come,
Let all doubts be dumb;
Let all words be mild,
All strifes be reconciled,
All pains beguiled;
Light brings no blindness,
Love no unkindness,
Knowledge no ruin,
Fear no undoing.
From the cradle to the grave,
Save, O save!

THE SPREADING SPECK.

W. R. ALGER'S "POETRY OF THE EAST."

On every human soul there lies
A little dusky speck of sin,
As small as a mote's eye in size:
But when that speck doth once begin

To work, it swift and swift extends,
Till the whole soul it comprehends,
And all its powers overclouds
With condemnation's thunder-shrouds.
Then fierce and far the fear-fires flash,
And dire and dread the doom-bolts dash.
Thus doth the sin-speck spread, in sight,
O'er all the soul a baleful night, —
A blotting night of horror deep,
That knows no dawn and knows no sleep!

LINES.

H. WARE, JR.

It is not what my hands have done,
  That weighs my spirit down,
That casts a shadow o'er the sun,
  And over earth a frown;
It is not any heinous guilt,
  Or vice by men abhorred;
For fair the fame that I have built,
  A fair life's just reward;
And men would wonder if they knew
How sad I feel with sins so few.

Alas! they only see in part,
  When thus they judge the whole;
They cannot look upon the heart,
  They cannot read the soul;
But I survey myself within,
  And mournfully I feel
How deep the principle of sin
  Its root may there conceal,
And spread its poison through the frame,
Without a deed that men can blame.

They judge by actions which they see
  Brought out before the sun;
But conscience brings reproach to me
  For what I 've left undone,—
For opportunities of good
  In folly thrown away,
For hours misspent in solitude,
  Forgetfulness to pray,—
And thousand more omitted things,
Whose memory fills my breast with stings.

And therefore is my heart oppressed
  With thoughtfulness and gloom;
Nor can I hope for perfect rest,
  Till I escape this doom.
Help me, thou Merciful and Just,
  This fearful doom to fly;

Thou art my strength, my hope, my trust;—
O help me lest I die!
And let my full obedience prove
The perfect power of faith and love.

A SUPPLICATION.

F. D. HUNTINGTON.

O Love Divine! lay on me burdens, if thou wilt;
Burdens to break in mercy my fond, feverish sleep;
Turn comforts into awful prophets to my guilt;
Let me but at thy wondrous footstool fall and weep!

Visit and change, uplift, ennoble, recreate me!
Ordain whatever masters in thy saving school;
Let the whole eager host of Fashion's votaries hate me,
So thou wilt henceforth guide me by thy loving rule.

I pray not, Lord, to be redeemed from mortal sorrow;
Redeem me only from my vain and mean self-love;

Then let each night of grief lead in a mourning
morrow,
Fear shall not shake my trust in Thee, — my
Peace above.

Yet while the Resurrection waves its signs au-
gust;
Like morning's dewy banners on a cloudless sky,
My weak feet cling enamored to the parching
dust,
And on the sand poor pebbles lure my roving
eye.

Ye witnesses of silent, sad Gethsemane, —
That shaded garden whence light breaks for all
our earth, —
Around my anguish let your faithful influence
be!
Ye prayers and sighs divine, be my immortal
birth!

Vales of repentance mount to hills of high de-
sire;
Seven times seven suffering years earn the sab-
batic rest;
Earth's fickle, cruel lap — alternate frost and
fire —
Tempers beloved disciples for the Master's
breast.

O Way for all that live! heal us by pain and loss;
Fill all our years with toil, and bless us with thy
rod.
Thy bonds bring wider freedom; climbing, by the
cross,
Wins that brave height where looms the city of
our God!

O Sunshine, rising ever on our nights of sadness!
O Best of all our good, and Pardoner of our sin!
Look down with pity on our unbelieving mad-
ness!
To heaven's great welcome take us, homesick
pilgrims, in!

Spirit that overcame the world's long tribulation!
Try faltering faith, and make it firm through
much enduring;
Feed weary hearts with patient hopes of thy sal-
vation;
Make strait submission, more than luxury's ease,
alluring.

Hallow our wit with prayer; our mastery steep
in meekness;
Pour on our study inspiration's holy light;
Hew out, for Christ's dear Church, a future with-
out weakness,
Quarried from thine eternal Beauty, Order, Might!

Met there, mankind's great brotherhood of souls
and powers,
Raise thou full praises from its farthest corners
dim ;
Pour down, O steadfast Sun! thy beams on all
its towers;
Roll through its world-wide spaces Faith's majestic hymn.

Come, age of God's own Truth, after man's age
of fables!
Seed sown in Eden, yield the nation's healing
tree!
Ebal and Sinai, Mamre's tent, the Hebrew tables,
All look towards Olivet, and bend to Calvary.

Fold of the tender Shepherd! rise, and spread!
Arch o'er our frailty roofs of everlasting strength!
Be all the body gathered to its living Head!
Wanderers we faint: O let us find our Lord at
length!

A HYMN.

O. W. WITHINGTON.

If, in its song to Thee, my hand alone
  Hath touched the harp, (my heart forgetting Thee,) —
If other feelings have inspired its tone
  Than such as thou might'st well approve in me, —
O give me grace, that when I wake again
Its chord, my soul may mingle in the strain!

I have been cold: O warm my heart, and stir
  Its better thoughts! I have been vain: renew
In me the feelings of a worshipper,
  Whose spirit longs to be more just and true.
Erring and weak, — Thou canst alone impart
Joy to my soul and sunshine to my heart.

THE SHRINE AND THE CONFESSIONAL.

C. G. FENNER.

"That good thinketh, good may do,
And God will help him thar to."
Castel of Love. 1250.

In the ruined Hall of Life,
Plunged in deep remorse, I sit;
Rent and shattered is the roof,
Trembling to its fall is it;
In rank, wild luxuriance
Has the ivy Habit clung
Round those mouldering buttresses,
And those ruined towers among.

Shattered strength and falling tower,—
Saints, once honored, now defaced,—
Streams the night-wind drear and cold
Where the shrine of old was placed.
O thou stern and awful wreck,
Desolate and waste and wild!
A callous man I stand again
Where once I knelt a pure young child.

And a dark and cowled form,
Slow, unmoving, sits and sighs:
Veiled its face,—I only see
Those earnest, dark, and mournful eyes.
Visitant, I know thy name;
Deep within my inmost heart

Thrills the pang that tells too well,
  Thou the Avenging Angel art.

While I gaze, the bitter tears
  Scalding fall from straining eyes;
Dread and anguish, startling fears,
  With the past stern memories rise.
I am sinful, frail, and weak,
  O my God, a child of dust!
I have sinned; O Spirit pure,
  Help me, for in thee I trust!

* * * * *

See that veiled form arise, —
  Back the gloomy cowl she throws!
Gentler beam those sad, soft eyes;
  From those lips how gently flows
Soothing speech of soothing power:
  "Mortal, dread me not, but hear;
The Angel of Repentance, I
  Bid thee look up, and never fear.

"Leave this ruined shrine, depart;
  Upward, onward, lies thy way;
Upward, with a cheerful heart,
  Onward, for 't is breaking day.
Thou hast dwelt in night too long;
  List those cheering notes, nor stay;
Hear the angels' morning song
  Bidding thee to duty's way."

Now the ruined hall is left;
  On life's highway glad I stand;
Behind me lies the desert waste.
  With free heart and ready hand
Now I grasp my pilgrim staff;
  Journey on, nor look behind,
Upward, onward, o'er the hills,
  Till my home in God I find!

HYMN AND PRAYER.

J. F. CLARKE.

INFINITE Spirit! who art round us ever,
  In whom we float, as motes in summer sky,
May neither life nor death the sweet bond sever,
  Which joins us to our unseen Friend on high.

Unseen, — yet not unfelt, — if any thought
  Has raised our mind from earth, or pure desire,
A generous act, or noble purpose brought,
  It is thy breath, O Lord, which fans the fire.

To me, the meanest of thy creatures, kneeling,
  Conscious of weakness, ignorance, sin, and
    shame,

Give such a force of holy thought and feeling,
  That I may live to glorify thy name;

That I may conquer base desire and passion,
  That I may rise o'er selfish thought and will,
O'ercome the world's allurement, threat, and fashion,
  Walk humbly, softly, leaning on thee still.

I am unworthy. — Yet for their dear sake
  I ask, whose roots planted in me are found,
For precious vines are propped by rudest stake,
  And heavenly roses fed in darkest ground.

Beneath my leaves, though early fallen and faded,
  Young plants are warmed, they drink my branches' dew.
Let them not, Lord, by me be Upas-shaded;
  Make me for their sake firm, and pure, and true.

For their sake too, the faithful, wise, and bold,
  Whose generous love has been my pride and stay,
Those who have found in me some trace of gold,
  For their sake purify my lead and clay.

And let not all the pains and toil be wasted,
  Spent on my youth by saints now gone to rest,

Nor that deep sorrow my Redeemer tasted
When on his soul the guilt of man was pressed.

Tender and sensitive, he braved the storm,
That we might fly a well-deserved fate,
Poured out his soul in supplication warm,
Looked with his eyes of love on eyes of hate.

Let all this goodness by my mind be seen,
Let all this mercy on my heart be sealed;
Lord, if thou wilt, thy power can make me clean!
O speak the word, — thy servant shall be healed!

A MEDITATION.

CHARLES J. FOX.*

"O FOR some special Providence!
O for some miracle!"
Thus cry our ingrate hearts, nor feel,
Father! thou lov'st us well;
Thou giv'st the seasons in their course,
The rain and sweet sunshine;
And air, and food, and light, and life,
Are constant gifts of thine.

* Of Nashua, N. H. These verses were written a few days before his death.

When health is bounding in each vein,
  And vigor nerves each limb,
On the praise-altar of our hearts
  How soon the fire grows dim!
But when come sickness and distress,
  And human aid is vain,
At once we light the incense-cup,
  And kneel to God again.

When all the friends we love the most
  Return our hearts' caress,
And life is full of joy and hope, —
  Then we forget to bless:
But if some loved one pines, and Death
  Seems hovering in the air,
O, how we wrestle for his life,
  With fasting and with prayer!

When fortune wears a smiling face,
  And all is sunny-hued,
When all around we see no cloud,
  How weak our gratitude!
But if misfortune's storm beats fierce
  On our devoted breasts,
We strive until by penitence
  God's rainbow on us rests.

'T is ever thus; — God's daily gifts
  Wake but a feeble lay;

We feel not, know not, how to prize,
  Till they have passed away.
Then, then, too late, we see Heaven's glow
  Upon their upward track,
And find that angels have been here.
  And try to hold them back.

Lord! if thou wert not perfect love,
  How could we be forgiven?
Scarce greater sin was his who fell,
  The Morning Star, from heaven;
Keep us from such ingratitude,
  While pilgrims here we roam,
Till thou shalt send thine angel down
  To guide our spirits home!

HYMN IN SICKNESS.

H. WARE, JR.

Father, thy gentle chastisement
  Falls kindly on my burdened soul;
I see its merciful intent,
  To warn me back to thy control;
And pray, that, while I kiss the rod,
I may find perfect peace with God.

The errors of my heart I know;
  I feel my deep infirmities;
For often virtuous feelings glow,
  And holy purposes arise,
But, like the morning clouds, decay,
As empty, though as fair, as they.

Forgive the weakness I deplore;
  And let thy peace abound in me,
That I may trust my heart no more,
  But wholly cast myself on thee.
O let my Father's strength be mine,
And my devoted life be thine!

THE PILGRIM AT HEAVEN'S GATE.

C. G. FENNER.

Casta placent Superis
Pura cum veste venite.
England's Helicon. 1600.

My Robe of Life is travel-worn,
  And dusty with the dusty way;
It beareth marks of many a storm,
  It beareth marks of many a fray, —
The morning shower, the damp night-dews,
Have left their dark, discoloring hues.

My Robe of *Life* is scorched and burnt
 By madly rushing through the fires,
Where sternest teachings I have learnt
 From passionate and fell desires;
Yet not without the loss of chaste
White innocence, no more replaced.

My Robe of Life is blood-besprent, —
 For though I never raised the knife
To smite my brother's breast, I 've sent
 A sharper steel through his soul's life,
And made his heart to bleed by deep
And angry words that murdered sleep.

My Robe of Life is tear-bedewed, —
 Tears wrung from mine and others' eyes,
That I so oft have shunned the good,
 That ever round us, God-sent, lies,
And tears by deeper anguish forced
From consciousness of virtue lost.

My Robe of Life is sin-bespotted,
 And much bewrayed by anxious care,
And here and there grown thin and rotted
 Away by too much wear and tear, —
And torn by thorny thickets, when
Through them I sought the road again.

My Robe of Life at first was fair
 And spotless as the driven snow,

'T was flung around me gently there
  Where spirits first from Heaven do go;
And, white and clean, it seemed to be
A type of God's own purity.

O Angel at the Heavenly Gate,
  How can I hope to enter, when
At that high portal, lone and late,
  At closing eve I come again,
After my life-day spent and past,
With this worn life-robe round me cast?

I hear a voice that, soft and low,
  Bids me to him, my Saviour, fly,
And he will cleanse as white as snow
  Or whitest wool this robe, and I
From him a wedding-robe shall have,
When this is mouldered in the grave.

A wedding-garment, brighter far
  Than that I did at first receive,
Brighter than gleam of silvery star,
  My Saviour, Christ, to me will give;
And flinging off Life's Robe, will I
Put on my Immortality.

THE STUDENT.

SACRED OFFERING.

"He knelt down by my bed, and prayed. My soul was thrilled by the sound of that voice, so familiar, and so loved, and a thousand tender recollections crowded upon my mind. I was refreshed and strengthened as I listened, and lifted nearer to heaven."

Jotham Anderson.

I ROSE in all the pride of youth,
To hail the light that round me lay;
Thirsting for knowledge and for truth,
My soul sprang on her heavenly way;
In vain the mysteries of the past,
Still sealed, before my eyes were cast.

I proudly thought to lift that veil
Which holier hearts than mine had tried,
Who, with long years of study pale,
Still found their loftier faith defied:
'T is mine! I cried, that meed to gain;—
Alas! that dream! how fond and vain!

An eye above beheld my pride,
As bending o'er the midnight oil,
How earthly and unsanctified
The motives that still urged my toil;
How in that unseen mental strife,
I wasted power, and health, and life.

Yes! mortal glory shone around,
  Its beams seemed kindling o'er my brow;
I thought my youth's long sufferings crowned,
  The hour of struggle over now:
But He above the incense spurned
Which with an earthly splendor burned.

With holier aims and purer fires
  He bade my spirit seek his shrine,
Resign to him my heart's desires,
  And raise them to a crown divine;
And in humility and tears
He bade me walk my future years.

That chastening hand soon laid me low;
  Imagination, wisdom, power, —
What were they in my overthrow?
  Oh! could they soothe my dying hour?
A still, small voice was whispering there,
"Thy pride is fallen, — thy hope is prayer."

The weight of death lay on my heart,
  My trembling lips refused to pray,
As, one by one, I saw depart
  The trusts of that aspiring day;
Confused and stricken, then I sought
Some anchor for my parting thought.

And I was not forsaken. He
  I served so faithlessly was near;

His pitying eye was over me,
   And marking every secret fear;
And in that hour of wild alarms
He gave a parent to my arms.

The aged knees for me were bent;
   I heard the voice so long beloved;
A calm into my soul was sent,
   And every sense was sweetly moved;
For tender memories thronged around
Again at that familiar sound.

I wept, and all my weakness owned, —
   Those sacred words unbound my grief;
The truth, the way, the life, I found,
   As on His breast I sought relief,
And owned, subdued, the light of heaven
To humble hearts alone is given.

HYMN.

J. BOWRING.

From the recesses of a lowly spirit
My humble prayer ascends. O Father! hear
Upsoaring on the wings of fear and meekness,
      Forgive its weakness.

I know, I feel, how mean and how unworthy
The trembling sacrifice I pour before thee;
What can I offer in thy presence holy,
But sin and folly?

For in thy sight, who every bosom viewest,
Cold are our warmest vows, and vain our truest;
Thoughts of a hurrying hour, our lips repeat them,
Our hearts forget them.

We see thy hand, — it leads us, it supports us;
We hear thy voice, — it counsels and it courts us;
And then we turn away, — and still thy kindness
Pardons our blindness.

And still thy rain descends, thy sun is glowing,
Fruits ripen round, flowers are beneath us blowing,
And, as if man were some deserving creature,
Joy covers nature.

O how long-suffering, Lord! but thou delightest
To win with love the wandering, — thou invitest,
By smiles of mercy, not by frowns or terrors,
Man from his errors.

Who can resist thy gentle call, appealing
To every generous thought, and grateful feeling?

That voice paternal, whispering, watching ever?
My bosom? — Never!

Father and Saviour! plant within that bosom
These seeds of holiness, and bid them blossom
In fragrance and in beauty bright and vernal,
And spring eternal.

Then place them in those everlasting gardens,
Where angels walk, and seraphs are the wardens;
Where every flower that creeps through death's
dark portal
Becomes immortal.

THE GATE OF HEAVEN.

DISCIPLES' HYMN-BOOK.

She stood outside the gate of heaven, and saw
them entering in,
A world-long train of shining ones, all washed
in blood from sin.

The hero-martyr in that blaze uplifted his strong
eye,
And trod firm the reconquered soil of his na-
tivity!

And he who had despised his life, and laid it
down in pain,
Now triumphed in its worthiness, and took it up
again.

The holy one, who had met God in desert cave
alone,
Feared not to stand with brethren around the
Father's throne.

They who had done, in darkest night, the deeds
of light and flame,
Circled with them about as with a glowing halo
came.

And humble souls, who held themselves too dear
for earth to buy,
Now passéd through the golden gate, to live
eternally.

And when into the glory the last of all did
go,
"Thank God! there *is* a heaven," she cried,
"though mine is endless woe."

The angel of the golden gate said: "Where, then,
dost thou dwell?
And who art thou that enterest not?" — "A
soul escaped from hell."

"Who knows to bless with prayer like thine, in hell can never be;
God's angel could not, if he would, bar up this door from thee."

She left her sin outside the gate, she meekly entered there,
Breathed free the blessed air of heaven, and knew her native air.

PART VII.

TRUST AND SUBMISSION.

ACTION AND THOUGHT.

R. M. MILNES.

There is a world where struggle and stern toil
Are all the nurture of the soul of man,—
Ordained to raise from life's ungrateful soil
Pain as he must, and Pleasure as he can.
Then to that other world of thought from this
Turns the sad soul, all hopeful of repose,
But round in weirdest metamorphosis,
False shapes and true, divine and devilish, close.
Above these two, and resting upon each
A meditative and compassionate eye,
Broodeth the Spirit of God; thence evermore,
On those poor wanderers, cast from shore to shore,
Falleth a voice, omnipotent to teach
Them that will hear,—"Despair not! it is I."

FROM "THE HEAVENLY FRIEND."

BERNARD BARTON.

THERE is A FRIEND more tender, true
Than brother e'er can be;
Who, when all others bid adieu,
Will still abide by thee;
Who, be their pathway bright or dim,
Deserts not those that turn to HIM.

The heart by Him sustained, though deep
Its anguish, still can bear;
The soul He condescends to keep,
Shall never know despair;
In nature's weakness, sorrow's night,
God is its strength, its joy, and light.

He is the Friend who changeth not
In sickness or in health,
Whether on earth our transient lot
Be poverty or wealth;
In joy or grief, contempt or fame,
To all who seek Him still the same.

Of human hearts He holds the key:
Is friendship meet for ours?
O, be assured that none but He
Unlocks its purest powers:

He can recall the lost, the dead,
Or give us nobler in their stead.

Of earthly friends, — who finds them true
May boast a happy lot;
But happier still, life's journey through,
Is he who needs them not:
A heavenly Friend, — to know we need,
To feel we have, — is bliss indeed.

A REMONSTRANCE

TO A FRIEND WHO COMPLAINED TO THE AUTHOR THAT HE WAS "ALL ALONE."

A. A. WATTS.

O, SAY not thou art all alone
Upon this wide, cold-hearted earth;
Sigh not o'er joys for ever flown, —
The vacant chair, the silent hearth:
Why should the world's unholy mirth
Upon thy quiet dreams intrude,
To scare those shapes of heavenly birth
That people oft thy solitude?

Though many a fervent hope of youth
  Hath passed, and scarcely left a trace;
Though earth-born love, its tears and truth,
  No longer in thy heart have place;
Nor time, nor grief can e'er efface
  The brighter hopes that now are thine,—
The fadeless love, all-pitying grace,
  That makes thy darkest hours divine!

Not all alone; for thou canst hold
  Communion sweet with saint and sage,
And gather gems, of price untold,
  From many a consecrated page:
Youth's dreams, the golden lights of age,
  The poet's lore, are still thine own;
Then, while such themes thy thoughts engage,
  O, how canst thou be all alone!

Not all alone; the lark's rich note,
  As, mounting up to heaven, she sings;
The thousand silver sounds that float
  Above, below, on morning's wings;
The softer murmurs twilight brings,—
  The cricket's chirp, cicada's glee;
All earth, that lyre of myriad strings,
  Is jubilant with life for thee!

Not all alone; the whispering trees,
  The rippling brook, the starry sky,

Have each peculiar harmonies
  To soothe, subdue, and sanctify:
The low, sweet breath of evening's sigh,
  For thee hath oft a friendly tone,
To lift thy grateful thoughts on high,
  And say, thou art not all alone!

Not all alone; a watchful Eye,
  That notes the wandering sparrow's fall,
A saving Hand, is ever nigh,
  A gracious Power attends thy call; —
When sadness holds the heart in thrall,
  Oft is His tenderest mercy shown;
Seek then the balm vouchsafed to all,
  And thou canst never be alone!

QUIET FROM GOD.

SACRED OFFERING.

"If he giveth quiet, who can make trouble?" — Job xxxiv. 29.

Quiet from God! It cometh not to still
  The vast and high aspirings of the soul, —
The deep emotions which the spirit fill,
  And speed its purpose onward to the goal;

It dims not youth's bright eye,
Bends not joy's lofty brow,
No guiltless ecstasy
Need in its presence bow.

It comes not in a sullen form, to place
Life's greatest good in an inglorious rest;
Through a dull, beaten track its way to trace,
And to lethargic slumber lull the breast:
Action may be its sphere,
Mountain paths, — boundless fields;
O'er billows its career:
This is the power it yields; —

To sojourn in the world, and yet apart;
To dwell with God, yet still with man to feel;
To bear about for ever in the heart
The gladness which His Spirit doth reveal;
Not to deem evil gone
From every earthly scene;
To see the storm come on,
But feel his shield between.

It giveth not a strength to human kind
To leave all suffering powerless at its feet,
But keeps within the temple of the mind,
A golden altar, and a mercy-seat,
A spiritual ark,
Bearing the peace of God,

Above the waters dark,
And o'er the desert's sod.

How beautiful within our souls to keep
This treasure, the All-merciful hath given;
To feel, when we awake, and when we sleep,
Its incense round us, like a breeze from heaven!
Quiet at heart and home,
Where the heart's joys begin;
Quiet where'er we roam,
Quiet around, within.

Who shall make trouble? Not the evil minds
Which like a shadow o'er creation lower.
The spirit peace hath so attuned finds
There feelings that may own the Calmer's power.
What may she not confer,
E'en where she must condemn?
They take not peace from her;
She may speak peace to them.

What shall make trouble? Not an adverse fate,
Not chilly poverty, nor worldly care;
They who are tending to a better state
Want but that peace to make them feel they are.
Care o'er life's little day
The tempest-cloud may roll;
Peace o'er its eve will play,
The moonlight of the soul.

Who shall make trouble? Not the holy thought
Of the departed, — that will be a part
Of those undying things which peace hath wrought
Into a world of beauty in the heart:
Not the forms passed away,
Which time's strong current bore;
The dark stream might not stay,
The ocean will restore.

Who shall make trouble? Not slow-wasting pain,
Not the impending, certain stroke of death;
These do but wear away, then snap the chain
Which bound the spirit down to things beneath.
The quiet of the grave
No trouble can destroy;
HE who is strong to save
Shall break it, — but with joy.

BALLAD OF THE TEMPEST.

J. T. FIELDS.

WE were crowded in the cabin,
Not a soul would dare to sleep, —
It was midnight on the waters,
And a storm was on the deep.

'T is a fearful thing in winter
To be shattered in the blast,
And to hear the rattling trumpet
Thunder, " Cut away the mast ! "

So we shuddered there in silence, —
For the stoutest held his breath,
While the hungry sea was roaring,
And the breakers talked with Death.

As thus we sat in darkness,
Each one busy in his prayers, —
" We are lost ! " the captain shouted,
As he staggered down the stairs.

But his little daughter whispered,
As she took his icy hand,
" Is n't God upon the ocean,
Just the same as on the land ? "

Then we kissed the little maiden,
And we spoke in better cheer,
And we anchored safe in harbor
When the morn was shining clear.

WRITTEN IN SICKNESS.

JOHN QUINCY ADAMS.

Lord of all worlds! let thanks and praise
To thee for ever fill my soul;
With blessings thou hast crowned my days,—
My heart, my head, my hand control:
O let no vain presumption rise,
No impious murmur in my heart,
To crave the boon thy will denies,
Or shrink from ill thy hands impart!

My soul, with endless being fraught,
Created by thy gracious laws,
With fancy, reason, judgment, thought,
The links between effect and cause,
Are gifts of goodness all divine,—
Sprung from the clod, to heaven they rise,
Immortal life with dust combine,
And blend in union earth and skies.

Life, health, and nurture to the boy
See from the mother's breast supplied;
Yet not for ever streams the joy,—
That flowing fountain must be dried:
Weaned, the fond mother's darling still
Without complaint bereavement bears,
No longer drains the milky rill,
But still the flood of bounty shares.

That child am I, and not an hour,
  Revolving in the orbs above,
But brings some token of thy power,
  But brings some token of thy love.
And shall this bosom dare repine,
  In darkness dare deny the dawn,
Or spurn the treasures of the mine,
  Because one diamond is withdrawn?

The fool denies, the fool alone,
  Thy being, Lord, and boundless might,
Denies the firmament thy throne,
  Denies the Sun's meridian light,
Denies the fashion of his frame,
  The voice he hears, the breath he draws:
O idiot atheist! to proclaim
  Effects unnumbered without cause!

Matter and mind, mysterious one,
  Are man's for threescore years and ten;
Where, ere the thread of life was spun?
  Where, when reduced to dust again?
All-seeing God! the doubt suppress, —
  The doubt thou only canst relieve;
My soul thy Saviour Son shall bless,
  Fly to thy Gospel, and believe.

"A LITTLE BIRD I AM."

WRITTEN IN PRISON.

MADAME GUYON.

A LITTLE bird I am,
  Shut from the fields of air;
And in my cage I sit and sing
  To Him who placed me there;
Well pleased a prisoner to be,
Because, my God, it pleases thee.

Naught have I else to do;
  I sing the whole day long;
And He whom most I love to please
  Doth listen to my song;
He caught and bound my wandering wing,
But still he bends to hear me sing.

Thou hast an ear to hear,
  A heart to love and bless;
And though my notes were ne'er so rude,
  Thou would'st not hear the less;
Because thou knowest, as they fall,
That Love, sweet Love, inspires them all.

My cage confines me round;
  Abroad I cannot fly;

But though my wing is closely bound,
  My heart 's at liberty.
My prison walls cannot control
The flight, the freedom of the soul.

O, it is good to soar
  These bolts and bars above,
To Him whose purpose I adore,
  Whose providence I love!
And in Thy mighty will to find
The joy, the freedom, of the mind.

THE ALPINE CROSS.

J. T. FIELDS.

Benighted once where Alpine storms
Have buried hosts of martial forms,
Halting with fear, benumbed with cold,
While swift the avalanches rolled,
Shouted our guide, with quivering breath,
"The path is lost! to move is death!"

The savage snow-cliffs seemed to frown,
The howling winds came fiercer down;
Shrouded in such a dismal scene,
No mortal aid whereon to lean,

Think you what music 't was to hear,
"I see the Cross! our way is clear!"

We looked, and there, amid the snows,
A simple cross of wood uprose.
Firm in the tempest's awful wrath,
It stood to guide the traveller's path,
And point to where the valley lies,
Serene beneath the summer skies.

One dear companion of that night
Has passed away from human sight.
He reached his home to droop and fade,
And sleep within his native glade;
But as his fluttering hand I took,
Before he gave his farewell look,
He whispered from his bed of pain,
"The Alpine cross I see again!"
Then, smiling, sank to endless rest,
Upon his weeping mother's breast.

PRISONS DO NOT EXCLUDE GOD.

MADAME GUYON.

Strong are the walls around me,
That hold me all the day;

But they who thus have bound me
  Cannot keep God away:
My very dungeon walls are dear,
Because the God I love is here.

They know, who thus oppress me,
  'T is hard to be alone;
But know not, One can bless me,
  Who comes through bars and stone:
He makes my dungeon's darkness bright,
And fills my bosom with delight.

Thy love, O God! restores me
  From sighs and tears to praise;
And deep my soul adores thee,
  Nor thinks of time or place:
I ask no more, in good or ill,
But union with thy holy will.

'T is that which makes my treasure,
  'T is that which brings my gain;
Converting woe to pleasure,
  And reaping joy from pain.
O, 't is enough, whate'er befall,
To know that God is All in All.

DE PROFUNDIS.

WILLIAM CROSWELL.

"There may be a cloud without a rainbow, but there cannot be a rainbow without a cloud."

My soul were dark
But for the golden light and rainbow hue
That, sweeping heaven with their triumphant arc,
Break on the view.

Enough to feel
That God indeed is good! enough to know
Without the gloomy clouds he could reveal
No beauteous bow.

"WHY THUS LONGING?"

MISS WINSLOW.

Why thus longing, thus for ever sighing
For the far-off, unattained, and dim;
While the beautiful, all round thee lying,
Offers up its low, perpetual hymn?

Wouldst thou listen to its gentle teaching,
All thy restless yearnings it would still;
Leaf and flower, and laden bee, are preaching,
Thine own sphere, though humble, first to fill.

Poor indeed thou must be, if around thee
  Thou no ray of light and joy canst throw;
If no silken cord of love hath bound thee
  To some little world through weal and woe;—

If no dear eyes thy fond love can brighten,
  No fond voices answer to thine own;
If no brother's sorrow thou canst lighten,
  By daily sympathy and gentle tone.

Not by deeds that win the crowd's applauses,
  Not by works that give thee world-renown,
Not by martyrdom or vaunted crosses,
  Canst thou win and wear the immortal crown.

Daily struggling, though unloved and lonely,
  Every day a rich reward will give;
Thou wilt find, by hearty striving only,
  And truly loving, thou canst truly live.

Dost thou revel in the rosy morning,
  When all nature hails the Lord of light,
And his smile, the mountain-tops adorning,
  Robes yon fragrant fields in radiance bright?

Other hands may grasp the field and forest,
  Proud proprietors in pomp may shine;
But with fervent love if thou adorest,
  Thou art wealthier,—all the world is thine!

Yet if through earth's wide domains thou rovest,
  Sighing that they are not thine alone,
Not those fair fields, but thyself thou lovest,
  And their beauty and thy worth are gone.

Nature wears the colors of the spirit;
  Sweetly to her worshipper she sings;
All the glow, the grace, she doth inherit,
  Round her trusting child she fondly flings.

THE POOR CHILD'S HYMN.

MARY HOWITT.

We are poor and lowly born;
  With the poor we bide;
Labor is our heritage,
  Care and want beside.
What of this? Our blessed Lord
  Was of lowly birth,
And poor, toiling fishermen
  Were his friends on earth!

We are ignorant and young;
  Simple children all;
Gifted with but humble powers,
  And of learning small.

What of this? Our blessed Lord
  Loved such as we;
How he blessed the little ones
  Sitting on his knee!

HOPE IS BETTER THAN EASE.

J. KEBLE. — CHRISTIAN YEAR.

"I desire that ye faint not at my tribulations for you, which is your glory." — Ephesians iii. 13.

Wish not, dear friends, my pain away, —
  Wish me a wise and thankful heart,
With God, in all my griefs, to stay,
  Nor from his loved correction start.

The dearest offering he can crave
  His portion in our souls to prove,
What is it to the gift he gave,
  The only Son of his dear love?

But we, like vexed, unquiet sprites,
  Will still be hovering o'er the tomb,
Where buried lie our vain delights,
  Nor sweetly take a sinner's doom.

In life's long sickness evermore
  Our thoughts are tossing to and fro:

We change our posture o'er and o'er,
  But cannot rest, nor cheat our woe.

Were it not better to lie still,
  Let Him strike home, and bless the rod, —
Never so safe as when our will
  Yields undiscerned by all but God?

Thy precious things, whate'er they be
  That haunt and vex thee, heart and brain,
Look to the cross, and thou shalt see
  How thou may'st turn them all to gain.

Lovest thou praise? the cross is shame;
  Or ease? the cross is bitter grief;
More pangs than tongue or heart can frame
  Were suffered there without relief.

We of that altar would partake,
  But cannot quit the cost, — no throne
Is ours, to leave for thy dear sake, —
  We cannot do as thou hast done.

We cannot part with heaven for Thee, —
  Yet guide us in thy track of love;
Let us gaze on where light should be,
  Though not a beam the clouds remove.

So wanderers ever fond and true
  Look homeward through the evening sky,

Without a streak of heaven's soft blue
 To aid affection's dreaming eye.

The wanderer seeks his native bower,
 And we will look and long for Thee,
And thank thee for each trying hour,
 Wishing, not struggling, to be free.

LINES.

OLIVER W. B. PEABODY.

O who that has gazed, in the stillness of even,
 On the fast fading hues of the west,
Has seen not afar, in the bosom of heaven,
 Some bright little mansion of rest,
And mourned that the path to a region so fair
 Should be shrouded with sadness and fears,—
That the night-winds of sorrow, misfortune, and care
Should sweep from the deep rolling waves of despair,
 To darken this cold world of tears?

And who that has gazed has not longed for the hour
 When misfortune for ever shall cease;

And Hope, like the rainbow, unfold through the shower
Her bright-written promise of peace?
And oh! if that rainbow of promise may shine
On the last scene of life's wintry gloom,
May its light in the moment of parting be mine;
I ask but one ray from a source so divine,
To brighten the vale of the tomb.

CONSOLATIONS.

HARRIET MARTINEAU.

Mourner! thou seekest Rest.
Rise from thy couch, and dry the tears unblest,
And sigh no more for blessings now resigned.
Go to the fount of life which ever flows;
There thou mayst gain oblivion of thy woes,
There shall thy spirit own a sweet repose.
Seek Rest, and thou shalt find.

Thou seekest Health; and how?
Let gloom and tears no more thy spirit bow;
Health springs aloft upon the viewless wind:
Up to the mountain-top pursue her flight;
Over the fresh turf track her footsteps light;
In hawthorn bowers, 'mid fountains gushing bright,
Seek her, and thou shalt find.

But Hope hath left thee too,
'Mid many griefs, and comforts all too few.
Think not her angel-presence is confined
To earth; but seek the helps which God hath given
To aid thy feeble sight, and through the heaven
See where she soars, bright as the star of even.
Then seek, and thou shalt find.

Dost thou seek Peace, and where?
'Mong thine own withered hopes? She is not there.
Nor in the depths of thine own darkened mind.
Lay thy heart open to the infant's mirth,
Send the bright hopes of others from their birth,
Look round for all that 's beautiful on earth.
Seek Peace, and thou shalt find.

Seek Peace and Hope and Rest:
And as the eagle flutters o'er her nest,*
And bears her young, all trembling, weak, and blind,
Up to heaven-gate on her triumphant wing, —
So shall the Lord thy God thy spirit bring
To whom eternal suns their radiance fling.
Him seek, and thou shalt find.

---

* Deuteronomy xxxii. 11.

PARAPHRASE OF PSALM XXII.

H. K. WHITE.

My God, my God, O why dost thou forsake me?
  Why art thou distant in the hour of fear?
To thee, my wonted help, I still betake me,
  To thee I clamor, but thou dost not hear.

The beam of morning witnesses my sighing,
  The lonely night-hour views me weep in vain;
Yet thou art holy, and on thee relying,
  Our fathers were released from grief and pain.

To thee they cried, and thou didst hear their wailing,
  On thee they trusted, and their trust was sure;
But I, poor, lost, and wretched son of failing,
  I, without hope, must scorn and hate endure.

Me they revile; with many ills molested,
  They bid me seek of thee, O Lord, redress:
On God, they say, his hope and trust he rested,
  Let God relieve him in his deep distress.

To me, Almighty, in thy mercy shining,
  Life's dark and dangerous portals thou didst ope;

And, softly on my mother's lap reclining,
  Breathed through my breast the lively soul of
      hope.

Even from the womb, thou art my God, my Father!
  Aid me, now trouble weighs me to the ground:
Me heavy ills have worn, and, faint and feeble,
  The bulls of Bashan have beset me round.

My heart is melted, and my soul is weary;
  The wicked ones have pierced my hands and
      feet!
Lord, let thy influence cheer my bosom dreary:
  My help! my strength! let me thy presence
      greet!

Save me! O, save me! from the sword dividing,
  Give me my darling from the jaws of death!
Thee will I praise, and, in thy name confiding,
  Proclaim thy mercies with my latest breath.

"TO WHOM SHALL WE GO?"

MRS. E. L. FOLLEN.

When our purest delights are nipt in the blossom,
  When those we love best are laid low,
When grief plants in secret her thorns in the bosom,
  Deserted, "to whom shall we go?"

When error bewilders, and our path becomes
dreary,
And tears of despondency flow;
When the whole head is sick, and the whole
heart is weary,
Despairing, "to whom shall we go?"

When the sad, thirsty spirit turns from the
springs
Of enchantment this life can bestow,
And sighs for another, and flutters its wings,
Impatient, "to whom shall we go?"

O blest be that light which has parted the clouds,
A path to the pilgrim to show,
That pierces the veil which the future enshrouds,
And shows us to whom we may go.

A PRAYER.

R. M. MILNES.

Evil, every living hour,
Holds us in its wilful hand,
Save as thou, essential Power,
Mayst be gracious to withstand:
Pain within the subtle flesh,
Heavy lids that cannot close,

Hearts that hope will not refresh, —
Hand of Healing! interpose.

Tyranny's strong breath is tainting
Nature's sweet and vivid air,
Nations silently are fainting,
Or up-gather in despair:
Not to those distracted wills
Trust the judgment of their woes;
While the cup of anguish fills,
Arm of Justice! interpose.

Pleasures night and day are hovering
Round their prey of weary hours,
Weakness and unrest discovering
In the best of human powers:
Ere the fond delusions tire,
Ere envenomed passion grows
From the root of vain desire, —
Mind of Wisdom! interpose.

Now no more in tuneful motion
Life with love and duty glides;
Reason's meteor-lighted ocean
Bears us down its mazy tides;
Head is clear and hand is strong,
But our heart no haven knows;
Sun of Truth! the night is long, —
Let thy radiance interpose!

GOD RULING IN ALL.

ALFRED TENNYSON. — IN MEMORIAM.

Love is and was my Lord and King,
And in his presence I attend
To hear the tidings of my friend,
Which every hour his couriers bring.

Love is and was my King and Lord,
And will be, though as yet I keep
Within his court on earth, and sleep
Encompassed by his faithful guard,

And hear at times a sentinel
That moves about from place to place,
And whispers to the vast of space
Among the worlds, that all is well.

And all is well, though faith and form
Be sundered in the night of fear;
Well roars the storm to those that hear
A deeper voice across the storm,

Proclaiming social truth shall spread,
And justice, e'en though thrice again
The red fool-fury of the Seine
Should pile her barricades with dead.

A CHRISTMAS CAROL.

CHARLES KINGSLEY.

It chanced upon the merry, merry Christmas eve
I went sighing past the church, across the moorland dreary, —
"Oh! never sin and want and woe this earth will leave,
And the bells but mock the wailing sound they sing so cheery.
How long, O Lord! how long before thou come again?
Still in cellar, and in garret, and on moorland dreary
The orphans moan, and widows weep, and poor men toil in vain,
Till the earth is sick of hope deferred, though Christmas bells be cheery."

Then arose a joyous clamor from the wild-fowl on the mere,
Beneath the stars, across the snow, like clear bells ringing,
And a voice cried: "Listen! Christmas carols even here!
Though thou be dumb, yet o'er their work the stars and snows are singing.

Blind! I live, I love, I reign; and all the nations through
With the thunder of my judgments even now are ringing;
Do thou fulfil thy work, but as yon wild-fowl do,
Thou wilt heed no less the wailing, yet hear through it angels' singing."

THE HOPE OF MAN.

T. W. HIGGINSON.

The past is dark with sin and shame,
The future dim with doubt and fear;
But, Father, yet we praise thy name,
Whose guardian love is always near.

For man has striven, ages long,
With faltering steps to come to thee,
And in each purpose high and strong
The influence of thy grace could see.

He could not breathe an earnest prayer,
But thou wast kinder than he dreamed,
As age by age brought hopes more fair,
And nearer still thy kingdom seemed.

But never rose within his breast
  A trust so calm and deep as now ; —
Shall not the weary find a rest ?
  Father, Preserver, answer thou !

'T is dark around, 't is dark above,
  But through the shadow streams the sun ;
We cannot doubt thy certain love,
  And man's true aim shall yet be won !

PRAYER.

R. M. MILNES.

In reverence will we speak of those that woo
The ear Divine with clear and ready prayer ;
And, while their voices cleave the Sabbath air,
Know their bright thoughts are winging heaven-
    ward too.
Yet many a one, — the " latchet of whose shoe "
These might not loose, — will often only dare
Lay some poor words between him and despair,—
" Father, forgive ! we know not what we do."
For, as Christ prayed, so echoes our weak heart,
Yearning the ways of God to vindicate,

But worn and wildered by the shows of fate,
Of good oppressed and beautiful defiled,
Dim alien force, that draws or holds apart
From its dear home that wandering spirit-child.

HYMN.

W. H. HURLBURT.

We will not weep, — for God is standing by us,
And tears will blind us to the blessed sight;
We will not doubt; if darkness still doth try us,
Our souls have promise of serenest light.

We will not faint; if heavy burdens bind us,
They press no harder than our souls can bear;
The thorniest way is lying still behind us;
We shall be braver for the past despair.

O, not in doubt shall be our journey's ending,
Sin with its fears shall leave us at the last;
All its blest hopes in glad fulfilment blending,
Life shall be with us when the death is past.

Help us, O Father! when the world is pressing
On our frail hearts, that faint without their friend;
Help us, O Father! let thy constant blessing
Strengthen our weakness, — till the joyful end.

THE DEAD CHURCH.

CHARLES KINGSLEY.

Wild, wild wind, wilt thou never cease thy sighing?
Dark, dark night, wilt thou never wear away?
Cold, cold church, in thy death sleep lying,
Thy Lent is past, thy Passion here, but not thine Easter-day.

Peace, faint heart, though the night be dark and sighing;
Rest, fair corpse, where thy Lord himself hath lain.
Weep, dear Lord, where thy bride is lying;
Thy tears shall wake her frozen limbs to life and health again.

HOPE, DOUBT, AND TRUST.

ALFRED TENNYSON. — "IN MEMORIAM."

O, yet we trust that somehow good
Will be the final goal of ill,
To pangs of nature, sins of will,
Defects of doubt and taints of blood;

That nothing walks with aimless feet;
    That not one life shall be destroyed,
    Or cast as rubbish to the void,
When God hath made the pile complete;

That not a worm is cloven in vain;
    That not a moth with vain desire
    Is shrivelled in a fruitless fire,
Or but subserves another's gain.

Behold! we know not anything;
    I can but trust that good shall fall
    At last,—far off,—at last, to all,
And every winter change to spring.

So runs my dream: but what am I?
    An infant crying in the night:
    An infant crying for the light:
And with no language but a cry.

The wish, that of the living whole
    No life may fail beyond the grave,—
    Derives it not from what we have
The likest God within the soul?

Are God and Nature then at strife,
That Nature lends such evil dreams?
So careful of the type she seems,
So careless of the single life;

That I, considering everywhere
Her secret meaning in her deeds,
And finding that of fifty seeds
She often brings but one to bear;

I falter where I firmly trod,
And falling with my weight of cares
Upon the great world's altar-stairs,
That slope through darkness up to God;

I stretch lame hands of faith, and grope,
And gather dust and chaff, and call
To what I feel is Lord of all,
And faintly trust the larger hope.

THE MILLENNIUM.

COWPER.

O scenes surpassing fable, and yet true,
Scenes of accomplished bliss! which who can see,
Though but in distant prospect, and not feel
His soul refreshed with foretaste of the joy?
Rivers of gladness water all the earth,
And clothe all climes with beauty: the reproach
Of barrenness is past. The fruitful field
Laughs with abundance; and the land, once lean
Or fertile only in its own disgrace,
Exults to see its thirsty curse repealed.
The various seasons woven into one,
And that one season an eternal spring,
The garden fears no blight, and needs no fence,
For there is none to covet, all are full.
The lion, and the libbard, and the bear,
Graze with the fearless flocks; all bask at noon,
Together, or all gambol in the shade
Of the same grove, and drink one common stream.
Antipathies are none. No foe to man
Lurks in the serpent now: the mother sees,
And smiles to see, her infant's playful hand
Stretched forth to dally with the crested worm,
To stroke his azure neck, or to receive

The lambent homage of his arrowy tongue.
All creatures worship man, and all mankind
One Lord, one Father. Error has no place:
That creeping pestilence is driven away:
The breath of Heaven has chased it. In the heart
No passion touches a discordant string,
But all is harmony and love. Disease
Is not: the pure and uncontaminate blood
Holds its due course, nor feels the frost of age.
One song employs all nations; and all cry,
"Worthy the Lamb, for he was slain for us!"
The dwellers in the vales and on the rocks
Shout to each other, and the mountain-tops
From distant mountains catch the flying joy;
Till, nation after nation taught the strain,
Earth rolls the rapturous Hosanna round.
Behold the measure of the promise filled;
See Salem built, the labor of a God!
Bright as a sun the sacred city shines;
All kingdoms and all princes of the earth
Flock to that light; the glory of all lands
Flows into her; unbounded is her joy,
And endless her increase. Thy rams are there,
Nebaioth, and the flocks of Kedar there:
The looms of Ormus, and the mines of Ind,
And Saba's spicy groves, pay tribute there.
Praise is in all her gates: upon her walls,
And in her streets, and in her spacious courts,
Is heard salvation. Eastern Java there

Kneels with the native of the farthest West;
And Ethiopia spreads abroad the hand,
And worships. Her report has travelled forth
Into all lands. From every clime they come
To see thy beauty, and to share thy joy,
O Sion! an assembly such as Earth
Saw never, such as Heaven stoops down to see.

PART VIII.

DEATH AND IMMORTALITY.

SONGS OF BEING.

SARGENT'S SELECTION.

THE BIRTH.

Hail! new-waked atom of the eternal whole,
  Young voyager upon Time's mighty river!
      Hail to thee, Human Soul!
        Hail, and for ever!
      Pilgrim of life, all hail!
  He who at first called forth
  From nothingness the earth,
Who clothed the hills in strength, and dug the sea,
    Who gave the stars to gem
    Night like a diadem,
      Thou little child, made thee;
    Young habitant of earth
Fair as its flowers, though brought in sorrow forth,
    Thou art akin to God who fashioned thee!

The heavens themselves shall vanish as a scroll,
The solid earth dissolve, the stars grow pale,
But thou, O Human Soul,
Shalt be immortal! Hail!
Thou young Immortal, Hail!
He, before whom are dim
Seraph and cherubim,
Who gave the archangels strength and majesty,
Who sits upon heaven's throne,
The Everlasting One,
Thou little child, made thee!
Fair habitant of earth,
Immortal in thy God, though mortal by thy birth,
Born for life's trials, hail! all hail to thee!

THE DEATH.

Shrink not, O Human Spirit!
The Everlasting Arm is strong to save!
Look up, look up, frail nature! put thy trust
In Him who went down mourning to the dust,
And overcame the grave!
Quickly goes down the sun;
Life's work is almost done;
Fruitless endeavor, hope deferred, and strife!
One little struggle more,
One pang, and then is o'er
All the long, mournful weariness of life.
Kind friends, 't is almost past;
Come now, and look your last!

Sweet children, gather near,
And his last blessing hear.
See how he loved you, who departeth now!
And, with thy trembling step and pallid brow,
O, most belovéd one,
Whose breast he leaned upon,
Come, faithful unto death,
Receive his parting breath!
The fluttering spirit panteth to be free, —
Hold him not back who speeds to victory!
— The bonds are riven, the struggling soul is free!

Hail, hail, enfranchised spirit!
Thou that the wine-press of the field hast trod!
On, blest Immortal, on through boundless space,
And stand with thy Redeemer, face to face,
And bow before thy God!
Life's weary work is o'er,
Thou art of earth no more, —
No more art trammelled by the oppressive clay,
But tread'st with wingéd ease
The high acclivities
Of truths sublime, up heaven's crystalline way.
Here is no bootless quest;
The city's name is Rest;
Here shall no fear appall;
Here love is all in all;
Here shalt thou win thy ardent soul's desire;
Here clothe thee in thy beautiful attire.

Lift, lift thy wondering eyes!
Yonder is Paradise,
And this fair shining band
Are spirits of thy land!
And these that throng to meet thee are thy kin,
Who have awaited thee, redeemed from sin!
The city gates unfold, — enter, O enter in!

TO NIGHT.

J. BLANCO WHITE.

Mysterious Night! when our first parent knew
Thee from report divine, and heard thy name,
Did he not tremble for this lovely frame,
This glorious canopy of light and blue?
Yet 'neath a curtain of translucent dew,
Bathed in the rays of the great setting flame,
Hesperus with the host of heaven came,
And lo! creation widened in man's view.
Who could have thought such darkness lay concealed
Within thy beams, O sun? or who could find,
Whilst fly, and leaf, and insect stood revealed,
That to such countless orbs thou mad'st us blind?
Why do we, then, shun death with anxious strife?
If light can thus deceive, wherefore not life?

A WALK IN A CHURCHYARD.

R. C. TRENCH.

WE walked within the churchyard bounds,
My little boy and I,—
He laughing, running happy rounds,
I pacing mournfully.

"Nay, child! it is not well," I said,
"Among the graves to shout,
To laugh and play among the dead,
And make this noisy rout."

A moment to my side he clung,
Leaving his merry play,
A moment stilled his joyous tongue,
Almost as hushed as they:

Then, quite forgetting the command,
In life's exulting burst
Of early glee, let go my hand,
Joyous as at the first.

And now I did not check him more,
For, taught by Nature's face,
I had grown wiser than before,
Even in that moment's space.

She spread no funeral pall above
That patch of churchyard ground,
But the same azure vault of love
As hung o'er all around.

And white clouds o'er that spot would pass,
As freely as elsewhere;
The sunshine on no other grass
A richer hue might wear.

And formed from out that very mould
In which the dead did lie,
The daisy with its eye of gold
Looked up into the sky.

The rook was wheeling overhead,
Nor hastened to be gone, —
The small bird did its glad notes shed,
Perched on a gray headstone.

And God, I said, would never give
This light upon the earth,
Nor bid in childhood's heart to live
These springs of gushing mirth,

If our one wisdom were to mourn
And linger with the dead, —
To nurse, as wisest, thoughts forlorn
Of worm and earthy bed.

O no! the glory earth puts on,
  The child's unchecked delight,
Both witness to a triumph won,
  (If we but read aright,) —

A triumph won o'er sin and death, —
  From these the Saviour saves;
And, like a happy infant, Faith
  Can play among the graves.

THE CHILD AND THE MOURNERS.

C. MACKAY.

A LITTLE child beneath a tree
Sat and chanted cheerily
A little song, a pleasant song,
Which was, — she sang it all day long, —
"When the wind blows, the blossoms fall;
But a good God reigns over all!"

There passed a lady by the way,
Moaning in the face of day:
There were tears upon her cheek,
Grief in her heart too great to speak;
Her husband died but yester-morn,
And left her in the world forlorn.

She stopped and listened to the child,
That looked to heaven, and, singing, smiled;
And saw not for her own despair
Another lady, young and fair,
Who, also passing, stopped to hear
The infant's anthem ringing clear.

For she but few sad days before
Had lost the little babe she bore;
And grief was heavy at her soul
As that sweet memory o'er her stole,
And showed how bright had been the past,
The present drear and overcast.

And as they stood beneath the tree
Listening, soothed and placidly,
A youth came by, whose sunken eyes
Spake of a load of miseries;
And he, arrested like the twain,
Stopped to listen to the strain.

Death had bowed the youthful head
Of his bride beloved, his bride unwed:
Her marriage robes were fitted on,
Her fair young face with blushes shone,
When the destroyer smote her low,
And changed the lover's bliss to woe.

And these three listened to the song,
Silver-toned, and sweet, and strong,

Which that child, the livelong day,
Chanted to itself in play:
" When the wind blows, the blossoms fall;
But a good God reigns over all!"

The widow's lips impulsive moved;
The mother's grief, though unreproved,
Softened, as her trembling tongue
Repeated what the infant sung;
And the sad lover, with a start,
Conned it over to his heart.

And though the child — if child it were,
And not a seraph sitting there —
Was seen no more, the sorrowing three
Went on their way resignedly,
The song still ringing in their ears: —
Was it music of the spheres?

Who shall tell? They did not know,
But in the midst of deepest woe,
The strain recurred when sorrow grew,
To warn them, and console them too:
" When the wind blows, the blossoms fall;
But a good God reigns over all!"

LINES ADDRESSED TO A MOTHER, ON THE DEATH OF TWO INFANTS.

J. Q. ADAMS.

Sure, to the mansions of the blest
  When infant innocence ascends,
Some angel, brighter than the rest,
  The spotless spirit's flight attends.
On wings of ecstasy they rise
  Beyond where worlds material roll,
Till some fair sister of the skies
  Receives the unpolluted soul.
There, at the Almighty Father's hand,
  Nearest the throne of living light,
The choirs of infant seraphs stand,
  And dazzling shine, where all are bright.
Chained for a dreary length of years
  Down to these elements below,
Some stain the sky-born spirit bears
  Contracted from this world of woe.
That unextinguishable beam,
  With dust united at our birth,
Sheds a more dim, discolored gleam,
  The more it lingers upon earth.
Closed in this dark abode of clay,
  The stream of glory faintly burns;
Not unobscured, the lucid ray
  To its own native fount returns.

But when the Lord of mortal breath
  Decrees his bounty to resume,
And points the silent shaft of death
  Which speeds an infant to the tomb,
No passion fierce, nor low desire,
  Has quenched the radiance of the flame ;
Back to its God the living fire
  Reverts, unclouded as it came.
O Anna ! be that solace thine ;
  Let Hope her healing charm impart,
And soothe, with melodies divine,
  The anguish of a mother's heart.
O, think the darlings of thy love,
  Divested of this earthly clod,
Amid unnumbered saints above,
  Bask in the bosom of their God !
Of their *short* pilgrimage on earth
  Still tender images remain ;
Still, still they bless thee for their birth,
  Still, filial gratitude retain.
The days of pain, the nights of care,
  The bosom's agonizing strife,
The pangs which thou for them didst bear, —
  No ! they forget them not with life.
Scarce could their germing thought conceive,
  While in this vale of tears they dwelt,
Scarce their fond sympathy relieve
  The sufferance thou for them hast felt.
But there the soul's perennial flower
  Expands in never-fading bloom,

Spurns at the grave's poor transient hour,
  And shoots immortal from the tomb.
No weak, unformed idea there
  Toils, the mere promise of a mind;
The tide of intellect flows clear,
  Strong, full, unchanging, and refined.
Each anxious care, each rending sigh,
  That wrung for them the parent's breast,
Dwells on remembrance in the sky,
  Amid the raptures of the blest.
O'er thee with looks of love they bend,
  For thee the Lord of life implore,
And oft from sainted bliss descend,
  Thy wounded quiet to restore.
Oft in the stillness of the night
  They smooth the pillow for thy bed;
Oft, till the morn's returning light,
  Still watchful hover o'er thy head.
Hark! in such strains as saints employ,
  They whisper to thy bosom, Peace;
Calm the perturbed heart to joy,
  And bid the streaming sorrow cease.
Then dry henceforth the bitter tear,
  Their path and thine inverted see;
Thou wert *their* guardian angel here,
  They guardian angels now *to thee.*

TO A DYING INFANT.

MRS. L. H. SIGOURNEY.

Go to thy rest, my child!
  Go to thy dreamless bed,
Gentle and undefiled,
  With blessings on thy head;
Fresh roses in thy hand,
  Buds on thy pillow laid,
Haste from this fearful land,
  Where flowers so quickly fade.

Before thy heart might learn
  In waywardness to stray,
Before thy foot could turn
  The dark and downward way,
Ere sin might wound the breast,
  Or sorrow wake the tear,
Rise to thy home of rest,
  In yon celestial sphere.

Because thy smile was fair,
  Thy lip and eye so bright,
Because thy cradle care
  Was such a fond delight,
Shall Love, with weak embrace,
  Thy heavenward flight detain?
No! Angel, seek thy place
  Amid yon cherub train.

LITTLE CHARLIE.

HORATIO ALGER, JR.

A VIOLET grew by the river-side,
And gladdened all hearts with its bloom;
While over the fields, on the scented air,
It breathed a rich perfume.
But the clouds grew dark in the angry sky,
And its portals were opened wide;
And the heavy rain beat down the flower
That grew by the river-side.

Not far away, in a pleasant home,
There lived a little boy,
Whose cheerful face and childish grace
Filled every heart with joy.
He wandered one day to the river's verge,
With no one near to save;
And the heart that we loved with a boundless love
Was stilled in the restless wave.

The sky grew dark to our tearful eyes,
And we bade farewell to joy;
For our hearts were bound by a sorrowful tie
To the grave of the little boy.
The birds still sing in the leafy tree
That shadows the open door;
We heed them not, for we think of the voice
That we shall hear no more.

We think of him at eventide,
  And gaze on his vacant chair
With a longing heart, that will scarce believe
  That Charlie is not there.
We seem to hear his ringing laugh,
  And his bounding step at the door;
But alas! there comes the sorrowful thought,—
  We shall never hear them more!

We shall walk sometimes to his little grave,
  In the pleasant summer hours;
We will speak his name in a softened voice,
  And cover his grave with flowers;
We will think of him in his heavenly home,—
  His heavenly home so fair;
And we will trust with a hopeful trust
  That we shall meet him there.

TO J. S.

WILLIAM W. STORY.

" Better is the sight of the eyes, than the wandering oi the desire."
— Ecclesiastes vi. 9.

I YIELD thee unto higher spheres;
  I bend my head and say, " Thy will,
Not mine, be done," though bitter tears
  The while mine eyelids fill.

I know thou hast escaped the blight
  That wilts us here, and entered now
To perfect day, — though in the night
  Bereft of thee we bow.

And yet thy little sunny life
  Was beautiful as it was brief;
It was not vexed by pain or strife,
  It knew but little grief.

The sunshine from our house is gone,
  And from our hearts their peace and joy;
We feel so terribly alone
  Without thee, dearest boy!

Thou mad'st us feel how very fair
  God's earth could be, and taught us love;
And in life's tapestry of care
  A golden figure wove.

Brave as we will our hearts to bear,
  Grief will not wholly be denied;
The ineffectual dikes we rear
  Go down before its tide.

We lie all prostrate, — cannot feel
  God's love; we only cry aloud,
"O God! O God!" for all things reel,
  And God hides in a cloud.

We blindly wail, for we are maimed
  Beyond repair, until at last
He lifts us up, — all bleeding, lamed,
  And shattered by the blast.

He asks, "And would you wish him back,
  Whom I have taken to my joy, —
Drag downward to life's narrow track
  Your little spirit boy?"

"No! no!" the spirit makes reply, —
  "Not back to earthly chance and pain";
"Yet ah!" the shattered senses cry,
  "Would he were here again!"

He was so meshed within our love
  That all our heart-strings bleeding lie,
And all fond hopes we round him wove
  Are now but agony.

Yet let us suffer; he is freed,
  And on our tears a bridge of light
Is built by God, his steps to lead
  To joys beyond our sight.

LITTLE HERBERT.

MRS. S. F. CLAPP.

GATHER all his playthings up;
We shall never see them more,
From his dimpled, dainty hands,
Wildly thrown about the floor.

He is weary of them all,
Cares no more with them to play;
Leaving them, he hallows them:
Lay them lovingly away.

He hath heard the words of blessing,
Bidding little children, "Come";
Earthly love cannot detain him
Longer from his heavenly home.

Fold his little snowy hands
Lay them gently on his breast;
Now he lieth still and calm,—
Vision fair of perfect rest.

Bless him in his beauty there,—
Bless his solemn slumber deep;
"God's beloved," early crowned
With the mystic sign of "sleep." *

* "He giveth his beloved sleep."

Oft we prayed that angels might
Keep their watch about his bed:
We can trust their vigils now;
They will guard our infant dead.

While the silence in the house
Speaketh to us of our grief,
We will thank our God, who gave
Only for a season brief.

Mild and winning were his ways;
Very happy seemed he here;
Bright the sunshine that he brought
With him from the upper sphere.

One brief year he blest our home,
Filled our hearts with light and love,
Added to our lives a joy
That can never more remove.

All his grace and innocence
Hath increased our being's store;
What God giveth once is ours, —
Ours, with him, for evermore.

Now, a little hand is pointing
Heavenward, as we journey on;
May it guide us, and receive us,
When our earthly work is done!

THE LENT JEWELS.

A JEWISH TALE.

R. C. TRENCH.

In schools of wisdom all the day was spent:
His steps at eve the Rabbi homeward bent,
With homeward thoughts which dwelt upon the wife
And two fair children who consoled his life.
She, meeting at the threshold, led him in,
And, with these words preventing, did begin:—
"Ever rejoicing at your wished return,
Yet am I most so now: for since this morn
I have been much perplexed and sorely tried
Upon one point which you shall now decide.
Some years ago, a friend into my care
Some jewels gave,—rich, precious gems they were;
But having given them in my charge, this friend
Did afterward nor come for them, nor send,
But left them in my keeping for so long,
That now it almost seems to me a wrong
That he should suddenly arrive to-day,
To take those jewels, which he left, away.
What think you? Shall I freely yield them back,
And with no murmuring,—so henceforth to lack
Those gems myself, which I had learned to see
Almost as mine for ever, mine in fee?"

"What question can be here? Your own true heart
Must needs advise you of the only part:
That may be claimed again which was but lent,
And should be yielded with no discontent.
Nor surely can we find herein a wrong,
That it was left us to enjoy so long."

"Good is the word," she answered; "may we now
And evermore that it is good allow!"
And, rising, to an inner chamber led,
And there she showed him, stretched upon one bed,
Two children pale: and he the jewels knew,
Which God had lent him, and resumed anew.

FROM "ISOBEL'S CHILD."

MRS. E. B. BROWNING.

O MOTHER, mother! loose thy prayer!
Christ's name hath made it strong!
It bindeth me, it holdeth me
With its most loving cruelty,

From floating my new soul along
  The happy heavenly air!
It bindeth me, it holdeth me
In all this dark, upon this dull
Low earth, by only weepers trod!
It bindeth me, it holdeth me!
Mine angel looketh sorrowful
  Upon the face of God.

"Mother, mother! can I dream
Beneath your earthly trees?
I had a vision and a gleam, —
I heard a sound more sweet than these
  When rippled by the wind.
Did you see the Dove, with wings
Bathed in golden glisterings
From a sunless light behind,
Dropping on me from the sky,
Soft as a mother's kiss, until
I seemed to leap, and yet was still?
Saw you how his love-large eye
Looked upon me mystic calms,
Till the power of his divine
Vision was indrawn to mine?

"O the dream within the dream!
I saw celestial places even.
O the vistas of high palms,
Making finites of delight

Though the heavenly infinite, —
Lifting up their green, still tops
  To the heaven of Heaven!
O the sweet life-tree that drops
Shade like light across the river
Glorified in its for ever
  Flowing from the Throne!
O the shining holinesses
Of the thousand, thousand faces
God-sunned by the throned ONE!
And made intense with such a love,
That, though I saw them turned above,
Each, loving, seemed for also me!
And, O the Unspeakable! the HE,
The manifest in secrecies,
Yet of mine own heart partaker!
With the overcoming look
Of one who hath been once forsook,
  And blesseth the forsaker.
Mother, mother! let me go
Toward the face that looketh so.
Through the mystic, winged Four,
Whose are inward, outward eyes
Dark with light of mysteries, —
And the restless evermore
"Holy, holy, holy," — through
The sevenfold Lamps that burn in view
Of cherubim and seraphim;
Through the four and twenty crowned

Stately elders, white around,—
Suffer me to go to Him!

"Is your wisdom very wise,
Mother, on the narrow earth?
Very happy, very worth
That I should stay to learn?
Are these air-corrupting sighs
Fashioned by unlearned breath?
Do the students' lamps that burn
All night, illumine death?
Mother, albeit this be so,
Loose thy prayer and let me go
Where that bright chief angel stands
Apart from all his brother bands,
Too glad for smiling; having bent
In angelic wilderment
O'er the depths of God, and brought
Reeling thence one only thought
To fill his whole eternity.
He the teacher is for me!
He can teach what I would know;—
Mother, mother, let me go!

"Can your poet make an Eden
  No winter will undo?
And light a starry fire, while heeding
  His hearth's is burning too?
Drown in music the earth's din,

And keep his own wild soul within
The law of his own harmony?
  Mother, albeit this be so
Let me to my Heaven go!
A little harp me waits thereby, —
A harp whose strings are golden all,
And tuned to music spherical,
Hanging on the green life-tree,
Where no willows ever be.
Shall I miss that harp of mine?
Mother, no! — the Eye divine
Turned upon it, makes it shine, —
And when I touch it, poems sweet
Like separate souls shall fly from it,
Each to an immortal fytte.
We shall all be poets there,
Gazing on the chiefest Fair!

"And love! earth's love! and *can* we love
Fixedly where all things move?
Can the sinning love each other?
    Mother, mother!
I tremble in thy close embrace, —
I feel thy tears adown my face, —
Thy prayers do keep me out of bliss, —
    O dreary earthly love!
Loose thy prayer, and let me go
To the place which loving is,
Yet not sad! and when is given

Escape to *thee* from this below,
Thou shalt behold me that I wait
For thee beside the happy gate;
And silence shall be up in heaven
To hear our meeting kiss."

The nurse awakes in the morning sun,
And starts to see beside her bed
The lady, with a grandeur spread,
Like pathos, o'er her face, as one
God-satisfied and earth-undone:—
The babe upon her arm was dead!
And the nurse could utter forth no cry,—
She was awed by the calm in the mother's eye.

"Wake, nurse!" the lady said;
"*We* are waking,—he and I,—
I on earth, and he in sky!
And thou must help me to o'erlay
With garment white this little clay,
Which needs no more our lullaby.

"I changed the cruel prayer I made,
And bowed my meekened face, and prayed
That God would do his will! and thus
He did it, nurse: He parted *us*.
And His sun shows victorious
The dead, calm face; and *I* am calm:
And Heaven is hearkening a new psalm.

This earthly noise is too anear,
Too loud, and will not let me hear
The little harp. My death will soon
Make silence."

And a sense of tune,
A satisfiëd love, meanwhile,
Which nothing earthly could despoil,
Sang on within her soul.

O you,
Earth's tender and impassioned few,
Take courage to intrust your love
To Him so Named, who guards above
Its ends, and shall fulfil;
Breaking the narrow prayers that may
Befit your narrow hearts, away
In His broad, loving will.

THE INFANT SPIRIT'S PRAYER.

LINES ADDRESSED TO A LADY WHO HAD LOST HER HUSBAND AND CHILD.

ANONYMOUS.

"In heaven their angels do always behold the face of my Father."

SILENCE filled the courts of heaven, hushed were angel harp and tone,
While a little new-born spirit knelt before the Eternal throne.
As his small white hands were lifted, clasped as if in earnest prayer,
And his voice in low, sweet murmurs rose like music on the air,
Light from the full fount of glory on his robes of whiteness glistened,
And the bright-winged seraphs round him bowed their radiant heads and listened.

"Lord, from thy world of glory here,
My heart turns fondly to another:
O Lord, our God! the Comforter,
Comfort, comfort my sweet mother!
Many sorrows hast thou sent her,
Meekly hath she drained the cup,
And the jewels thou hast lent her,
Unrepining, yielded up:
Comfort, comfort my sweet mother!

"Earth is growing lonely round her,
  Friend and lover hast thou taken;
Let her not, though clouds surround her,
  Feel herself by thee forsaken.
Let her think, while faint and weary,
  We are waiting for her here;
Let each thought that makes earth dreary
  Make the thought of heaven more dear.

"Saviour, thou, in nature human,
  Dwelt on earth a little child,
Pillowed on the breast of woman,
  Blessed Mary, undefiled.
Thou, who from thy cross of suffering
  Viewed thy mother's tearful face,
And bequeathed her to thy loved one,
  Bidding him to fill thy place,
Comfort, comfort my sweet mother!

"Thou, who, from the heavens descending,
  Tears and woes and suffering won;
Thou, who, nature's laws suspending,
  Gave the widow back her son;
Thou, who at the grave of Lazarus
  Wept with those who wept their dead;
Thou, who once in mortal anguish
  Bowed thine own anointed head,—
Comfort, comfort my sweet mother!"

The dove-like murmur died away upon the evening air,
Yet still the little suppliant knelt, with hands still clasped in prayer,
Still were the softly-pleading eyes turned to the sapphire throne,
While angel harp and angel voice rang out in mingling tone;
And as the choral numbers swelled by angel voices given,
High, loud, and clear the anthem rolled through all the courts of Heaven.
"He is the widow's God," it said, "who spared not his own Son."
The infant spirit bowed its head, — "Thy will, O God, be done!"

RESIGNATION.

H. W. LONGFELLOW.

There is no flock, however watched and tended,
 But one dead lamb is there!
There is no fireside, howsoe'er defended,
 But has one vacant chair!

The air is full of farewells to the dying,
And mournings for the dead;
The heart of Rachel, for her children crying,
Will not be comforted!

Let us be patient! These severe afflictions
Not from the ground arise,
But oftentimes celestial benedictions
Assume this dark disguise.

We see but dimly through the mists and vapors;
Amid these earthly damps,
What seem to us but sad, funereal tapers
May be heaven's distant lamps.

There is no Death! What seems so is transition;
This life of mortal breath
Is but a suburb of the life elysian,
Whose portal we call Death.

She is not dead, — the child of our affection, —
But gone unto that school
Where she no longer needs our poor protection,
And Christ himself doth rule.

In that great cloister's stillness and seclusion,
By guardian angels led,
Safe from temptation, safe from sin's pollution,
She lives whom we call dead.

Day after day we think what she is doing
    In those bright realms of air;
Year after year, her tender steps pursuing,
    Behold her grown more fair.

Thus do we walk with her, and keep unbroken
    The bond which nature gives,
Thinking that our remembrance, though unspoken,
    May reach her where she lives.

Not as a child shall we again behold her;
    For when with raptures wild
In our embraces we again enfold her,
    She will not be a child;

But a fair maiden, in her Father's mansion,
    Clothed with celestial grace;
And beautiful with all the soul's expansion
    Shall we behold her face.

And though at times, impetuous with emotion
    And anguish long suppressed,
The swelling heart heaves moaning like the ocean,
    That cannot be at rest, —

We will be patient, and assuage the feeling
    We may not wholly stay;
By silence sanctifying, not concealing,
    The grief that must have way.

LINES TO A BEREAVED PARENT.

MRS. MARIA LOWELL.

WHEN on my ear your loss was knelled,
  And tender sympathy upburst,
A little rill from memory swelled,
  Which once had soothed my bitter thirst.

And I was fain to bear to you
  Some portion of its mild relief,
That it might be as healing dew
  To steal some fever from your grief.

After our child's untroubled breath
  Up to the Father took its way,
And on our home the shade of death
  Like a long twilight haunting lay,

And friends came round with us to weep
  Her little spirit's swift remove,
This story of the Alpine sheep
  Was told to us by one we love: —

"They, in the valley's sheltering care,
  Soon crop the meadow's tender prime,
And when the sod grows brown and bare,
  The shepherd strives to make them climb

"To airy shelves of pastures green,
That hang along the mountain's side,
Where grass and flowers together lean,
And down through mist the sunbeams slide.

"But naught can tempt the timid things
That steep and rugged path to try,
Though sweet the shepherd calls and sings,
And seared below the pastures lie,—

"Till in his arms their lambs he takes,
Along the dizzy verge to go,
Then, heedless of the lifts and breaks,
They follow on o'er rocks and snow.

"And in those pastures lifted fair,
More dewy soft than lowland mead,
The shepherd drops his tender care,
And sheep and lambs together feed."

This parable, by nature breathed,
Blew on me as the south-wind free
O'er frozen brooks that float unsheathed
From icy thraldom to the sea.

A blissful vision through the night
Would all my happy senses sway,
Of the good shepherd on the height,
Or climbing up the stony way,

Holding *our* little lamb asleep;
  And, like the burden of the sea,
Sounded that voice along the deep,
  Saying, "*Arise and follow me!*"

BEREAVEMENT.

KEBLE. — LYRA INNOCENTIUM.

"The Lord gave Job twice as much as he had before."

I MARKED when vernal meads were bright,
  And many a primrose smiled,
I marked her, bright as morning light,
  A dimpled three years' child.

A basket on one tender arm
  Contained her precious store
Of spring-flowers in their freshest charm,
  Told proudly o'er and o'er.

The other wound with earnest hold
  About her blooming guide,
A maid who scarce twelve years had told:
  So walked they side by side.

One a bright bud, and one might seem
  A sister flower half blown.

Full joyous on their loving dream
  The sky of April shone.

The summer months swept by: again
  That loving pair I met.
On russet heath, and bowery lane.
  The autumnal sun had set,

And chill and damp that Sunday eve
  Breathed on the mourners' road,
That bright-eyed little one to leave
  Safe in the saints' abode.

Behind, the guardian sister came,
  Her bright brow dim and pale: —
O cheer thee, maiden! in His name
  Who stilled Jairus' wail!

Thou mourn'st to miss the fingers soft
  That held by thine so fast,
The fond appealing eye, full oft
  Toward thee for refuge cast.

Sweet toils, sweet cares, for ever gone!
  No more from stranger's face,
Or startling sound, the timid one
  Shall hide in thine embrace.

Thy first glad earthly task is o'er,
  And dreary seems thy way;

But what if nearer than before
  She watch thee even to-day?

What if henceforth, by Heaven's decree,
  She leave thee not alone,
But in her turn prove guide to thee
  In ways to angels known?

O yield thee to her whisperings sweet:
  Away with thoughts of gloom!
In love the loving spirits greet,
  Who wait to bless her tomb.

In loving hope with her unseen
  Walk as in hallowed air.
When foes are strong, and trials keen,
  Think, "What if she be there?"

DEATH OF THE NEW-BAPTIZED.

KEBLE. — LYRA INNOCENTIUM.

What purer, brighter sight on earth, than when
  The sun looks down upon a drop of dew,
Hid in some nook from all but angels' ken,
  And with his radiance bathes it through and through,

Then into realms too clear for our frail view
Exhales and draws it with absorbing love?
And what if Heaven therein give token true
Of grace that new-born dying infants prove,
Just touched with Jesus' light, then lost in joys above?

ON THE DEATH OF A BEAUTIFUL GIRL.

MRS. E. L. FOLLEN.

The young, the lovely, pass away,
Ne'er to be seen again;
Earth's fairest flowers too soon decay,
Its blasted trees remain.

Full oft we see the brightest thing
That lifts its head on high
Smile in the light, then droop its wing,
And fade away and die.

And kindly is the lesson given;
Then dry the falling tear:
They came to raise our hearts to heaven,
They go to call us there.

ON THE DEATH OF A YOUNG LADY.

S. G. BULFINCH.

Alas, sweet maid! hast thou so soon departed?
Thou of the bright smile and the speaking eye,
The good, the cheerful, and the gentle-hearted, —
Who could have thought that thou so soon shouldst die?

To die so young, when all was bright before thee,
When fond affection strewed thy path with flowers!
Who could have thought so dark a doom was o'er thee,
Fair being, formed for life's most radiant hours?

How shall we miss thee where thy voice was heard!
How, where thy smile hath shed its light around!
And where we listened to the holy word,
Dear friend, with thee, on yonder hallowed ground!

Yes; in the hour of happiness, a sigh,
Sweet girl! shall witness that thou still art near;

And many a season, as it hastens by,
  Shall bid the past in vivid light appear.

But there are those who mourn thee with a deep,
  A heavier sorrow than 't is ours to know, —
They who in childhood watched thy tranquil sleep,
  And smoothed the pillow for thy brow of snow.

Friends of the orphan! He who gave your treasure
  Has taken to himself the boon he gave;
The pure, the gentle one, it was his pleasure
  From earth's dark sufferings early thus to save.

Lament her not! There, where her lovely spirit
  Abides, she glows with other thoughts than ours.
Not all that earth's most favored ones inherit
  Could win her now to leave those heavenly
      bowers.

There may we join her, Father! when the day
  Of duty and of trial here is done;
When earthly hope and fear have passed away,
  And the bright morn of endless life begun.

THE DYING HEBREW'S PRAYER.

ANONYMOUS.

A HEBREW knelt in the dying light:
  His eye was dim and cold,
The hairs on his brow were silver white,
  And his blood was thin and old!
He lifted his looks to his latest sun,
  For he knew that his pilgrimage was done;—
And as he saw God's *shadow* there,
  His spirit poured itself in prayer.

"I come unto death's second birth,
  Beneath a stranger air,
A pilgrim on a dull, cold earth,
  As all my fathers were!
And men have stamped me with a curse,—
  I feel it is not *Thine;*
Thy mercy, like yon sun, was made
  On me—as them—to shine;
And therefore dare I lift mine eye,
  Through that, to Thee, before I die.

"In this great temple, built by Thee,
  Whose altars are divine,
Beneath yon lamp that ceaselessly
  Lights up thine own true shrine,

O take my latest sacrifice!
   Look down, and make this sod
Holy as that where, long ago,
   The Hebrew met his God!

" I have not caused the widow's tears,
   Nor dimmed the orphan's eye,
I have not stained the virgin's years,
   Nor mocked the mourner's cry:
The songs of Zion in mine ear
   Have ever been most sweet,
And always, when I felt Thee near,
   My 'shoes' were 'off my feet'!

" I have known Thee in the whirlwind,
   I have known Thee on the hill,
I have loved Thee in the voice of birds,
   Or the music of the rill!
I dreamt Thee in the shadow,
   I saw Thee in the light,
I heard Thee in the thunder-peal,
   And worshipped in the night!
All beauty, while it spoke of Thee,
   Still made my soul rejoice,
And my spirit bowed within itself,
   To hear thy 'still, small voice'!
I have not felt myself a thing
   Far from thy presence driven,
By flaming sword or waving wing
   Shut out from Thee and heaven!

"Must I the whirlwind reap, because
My father sowed the storm?
Or shrink — because *another* sinned —
Beneath Thy red right arm?
O, much of this we daily scan,
And much is all unknown;
But I will not take my curse from *man*,
I turn to Thee alone!
O, bid my fainting spirit live,
And what is dark reveal,
And what is evil, O forgive!
And what is broken, heal;
And cleanse my nature, from above,
In the deep Jordan of thy love.

"I know not if the Christian's heaven
Shall be the same as mine;
I only ask to be forgiven,
And taken home to thine!
I wander on a far, dim strand,
Whose mansions are as tombs,
And long to find the fatherland,
Where there are many homes! —
O, grant, of all yon starry thrones,
Some dim and distant star,
Where Judah's lost and scattered sons
May love Thee from afar!
Where all earth's myriad harps shall meet
In choral praise and prayer,

Shall Zion's harps — of old so sweet —
  Alone be wanting there?
Yet place me in thy lower seat,
  Though I — as now — be, there,
The Christian's scorn, the Christian's jest;
  But let me see and hear,
From some dim mansion in the sky,
Thy bright ones, and their melody!"

The sun goes down with sudden gleam;
And beautiful as a lovely dream,
    And silently as air,
The vision of a dark-eyed girl,
    With long and raven hair,
Glides in as guardian spirits glide,
And lo! is kneeling by his side,
As if her sudden presence there
Were sent in answer to his prayer!
(O, say they not that angels tread
Around the good man's dying bed?)
His child, his sweet and sinless child!
    And as he gazed on her,
He knew his God was reconciled,
    And this the messenger,
As sure as God had hung on high
The promise-bow before his eye!
Earth's purest hope thus o'er him flung
    To point his heavenward faith,

And life's most holy feeling strung
To sing him unto death!
And on his daughter's stainless breast
The dying Hebrew found his rest.

THE BURIAL AT SEA.

CHARLES SPRAGUE.

Spare him one little week, Almighty Power!
Yield to his father's house his dying hour;
Once more, once more let them who hold him dear
But see his face, his faltering voice but hear;
We know, alas! that he is marked for death,
But let his mother watch his parting breath;
O, let him die at home!

It could not be!
At midnight, on a dark and stormy sea,
Far from his kindred and his native land,
His pangs unsoothed by tender woman's hand,
The patient victim in his cabin lay,
And meekly breathed his blameless life away.

* * * * *

Wrapped in the raiment that it long must wear,
His body to the deck they slowly bear;

How eloquent, how awful in its power,
The silent lecture of death's Sabbath-hour!
One voice that silence breaks,—the prayer is said,
And the last rite man pays to man is paid;
The flashing waters mark his resting-place,
And fold him round in one long, cold embrace;
Bright bubbles for a moment sparkle o'er,
Then break, to be, like him, beheld no more;
Down, countless fathoms down, he sinks to sleep,
With all the nameless shapes that haunt the deep.

Rest, loved one, rest,—beneath the billow's swell,
Where tongue ne'er spoke, where sunlight never fell;
Rest,—till the God who gave thee to the deep
Rouse thee, triumphant, from the long, long sleep.
And you, whose hearts are bleeding, who deplore
That ye must see the wanderer's face no more,
Weep,—he was worthy of the purest grief;
Weep,—in such sorrow ye shall find relief;
While o'er his doom the bitter tear ye shed,
Memory shall trace the virtues of the dead;
These cannot die,—for you, for him, they bloom,
And scatter fragrance round his ocean tomb.

VERSES

SUGGESTED BY THE DECEASE OF THE REV. MR. WRIGHT OF BOSTON, MISSIONARY AT LIBERIA, WITH HIS LADY, IN 1833; BOTH IN THE BLOOM OF YOUTH.

B. B. THATCHER.

WEEP not for him! He but rose to his rest
  From his own dear land of the fervid line,
With the silvery sheaves of his dawn all gleaned
  Ere bright dews blazoned his noon's decline.
He shall toil with tears in the gloom of a dim,
Lone harvest no more: O weep not for him!

And weep not for her! They have laid the dust
  Of the early exile so softly away,
In the pleasant shade of the plantain-tree,
  That the Judgment Angels, who seek that day
The jewels of glory, will scarcely stir
So sweet a slumber: weep not for her!

Weep not! In the clime where the sinless meet,
  Lingers no lonely yearning for this, —
As the pilgrims mourned (and smiled the while)
  In dreams,* o'er the visions of vanished bliss.
No sorrow enters that radiant realm, —
No mourning, nor yearning: O weep not for them!

---

* Alluding to a passage in Mr. Wright's Journal of his Voyage to Liberia.

TO MY FRIEND, ON THE DEATH OF HIS SISTER.

J. G. WHITTIER.

THINE is a grief, the depth of which another
May never know;
Yet o'er the waters, O my stricken brother!
To thee I go.

I lean my heart unto thee, — sadly folding
Thy hand in mine, —
With even the weakness of my soul upholding
The strength of thine.

I never knew, like thee, the dear departed;
I stood not by
When, in calm trust, the pure and tranquil-hearted
Lay down to die.

And on thy ear my words of weak condoling
Must vainly fall:
The funeral bell which in thy heart is tolling
Sounds over all!

I will not mock thee with the poor world's common
And heartless phrase,
Nor wrong the memory of a sainted woman
With idle praise.

With silence only as their benediction
God's angels come,
Where in the shadow of a great affliction
The soul sits dumb!

Yet would I say what thy own heart approveth:
Our Father's will,
Calling to him, the dear one whom he loveth,
Is mercy still.

Not upon thee or thine the solemn angel
Hath evil wrought:
Her funeral anthem is a glad evangel
The good die not!

God calls our loved ones, but we lose not wholly
What He hath given;
They live on earth, in thought and deed, as truly
As in His heaven.

And she is with thee. In thy path of trial
She walketh yet.
Still with the baptism of thy self-denial
Her locks are wet.

Up, then, my brother! Lo, the fields of harvest
Lie white in view!
She lives and loves thee, and the God thou servest
To both is true.

Thrust in thy sickle! — England's toil-worn peasants
Thy call abide;
And she thou mourn'st, a pure and holy presence,
Shall glean beside!

THE TWO ANGELS.

H. W. LONGFELLOW.

Two angels, one of Life and one of Death,
Passed o'er the village as the morning broke;
The dawn was on their faces, and beneath,
The sombre houses hearsed with plumes of smoke.

Their attitude and aspect were the same,
Alike their features and their robes of white;
But one was crowned with amaranth, as with flame,
And one with asphodels, like flakes of light.

I saw them pause on their celestial way;
Then said I, with deep fear and doubt oppressed:
"Beat not so loud, my heart, lest thou betray
The place where thy beloved are at rest!"

And he who wore the crown of asphodels,
  Descending, at my door began to knock,
And my soul sank within me, as in wells
  The waters sink before an earthquake's shock.

I recognized the nameless agony,
  The terror and the tremor and the pain,
That oft before had filled and haunted me,
  And now returned with threefold strength again.

The door I opened to my heavenly guest,
  And listened, for I thought I heard God's voice,
And, knowing whatsoe'er he sent was best,
  Dared neither to lament nor to rejoice.

Then with a smile, that filled the house with light,
  "My errand is not Death, but Life," he said;
And, ere I answered, passing out of sight,
  On his celestial embassy he sped.

'T was at thy door, O friend! and not at mine,
  The angel with the amaranthine wreath,
Pausing, descended, and, with voice divine,
  Whispered a word that had a sound like Death.

Then fell upon the house a sudden gloom,
  A shadow on those features fair and thin;
And softly, from that hushed and darkened room,
  Two angels issued, where but one went in.

All is of God! If he but wave his hand,
  The mists collect, the rain falls thick and louc
Till with a smile of light on sea and land,
  Lo! he looks back from the departing cloud.

Angels of Life and Death alike are his;
  Without his leave, they pass no threshold o'er
Who, then, would wish or dare, believing this,
  Against his messengers to shut the door?

FOLLEN.

ON READING HIS ESSAY ON "THE FUTURE STATE."

J. G. WHITTIER.

Friend of my soul! — as with moist eye
  I look up from this page of thine,
Is it a dream that thou art nigh,
  Thy mild face gazing into mine?

That presence seems before me now,
  A placid heaven of sweet moonrise,
When, dew-like, on the earth below
  Descends the quiet of the skies; —

The calm brow through the parted hair,
  The gentle lips which knew no guile,
Softening the blue eye's thoughtful care
  With the bland beauty of their smile.

Ah me! — at times that last dread scene
  Of Frost and Fire and moaning Sea
Will cast its shade of doubt between
  The failing eyes of Faith, and thee.

Yet, lingering o'er thy charmed page,
  Where through the twilight air of earth,
Alike enthusiast and sage,
  Prophet and bard, thou gazest forth,

Lifting the Future's solemn veil,
  The reaching of a mortal hand
To put aside the cold and pale
  Cloud-curtains of the Unseen Land!

In thoughts which answer to my own,
  In words which reach my inward ear,
Like whispers from the void Unknown,
  I feel thy living presence here.

The waves which lull thy body's rest,
  The dust thy pilgrim footsteps trod,
Unwasted, through each change, attest
  The fixed economy of God.

Shall these poor elements outlive
 The mind whose kingly will they wrought?
Their gross unconsciousness survive
 Thy godlike energy of thought?

Thou livest, Follen! — not in vain
 Hath thy fine spirit meekly borne
The burden of Life's cross of pain,
 And the thorned crown of suffering worn.

Oh! while Life's solemn mystery glooms
 Around us like a dungeon's wall, —
Silent earth's pale and crowded tombs,
 Silent the heaven which bends o'er all! —

While day by day our loved ones glide
 In spectral silence, hushed and lone,
To the cold shadows which divide
 The living from the dread Unknown; —

While ever on the closing eye,
 And on the lip which moves in vain,
The seals of that stern mystery
 Their undiscovered trust retain; —

And only 'midst the gloom of death,
 Its mournful doubts and haunting fears,
Two pale, sweet angels, Hope and Faith,
 Smile dimly on us through their tears; —

'T is something to a heart like mine
  To think of thee as living yet;
To feel that such a light as thine
  Could not in utter darkness set.

Less dreary seems the untried way
  Since thou hast left thy footprints there,
And beams of mournful beauty play
  Round the sad angel's sable hair.

Oh! at this hour when half the sky
  Is glorious with its evening light,
And fair broad fields of summer lie
  Hung o'er with greenness in my sight; —

While through these elm-boughs wet with rain
  The sunset's golden walls are seen,
With clover bloom and yellow grain
  And wood-draped hill and stream between; —

I long to know if scenes like this
  Are hidden from an angel's eyes;
If earth's familiar loveliness
  Haunts not thy heaven's serener skies.

For sweetly here upon thee grew
  The lesson which that beauty gave,
The ideal of the Pure and True
  In earth and sky and gliding wave.

And it may be that all which lends
  The soul an upward impulse here,
With a diviner beauty blends,
  And greets us in a holier sphere.

Through groves where blighting never fell,
  The humbler flowers of earth may twine;
And simple draughts from childhood's well
  Blend with the angel-tasted wine.

But be the prying vision veiled,
  And let the seeking lips be dumb,—
Where even seraph eyes have failed,
  Shall mortal blindness seek to come?

We only know that thou hast gone,
  And that the same returnless tide
Which bore thee from us still glides on,
  And we who mourn thee with it glide.

On all thou lookest we shall look,
  And to our gaze erelong shall turn
That page of God's mysterious book
  We so much wish, yet dread, to learn.

With Him, before whose awful power
  Thy spirit bent its trembling knee,—
Who, in the silent greeting flower,
  And forest leaf, looked out on thee,—

We leave thee, with a trust serene
  Which Time, nor Change, nor Death can move,
While with thy childlike faith we lean
  On Him whose dearest name is Love!

LINES ON CHANNING.

MRS. L. J. HALL.

When sinks the sun, shall we forget
That but to us his beams are set?
When holy spirits pass away,
Shall we but weep o'er feeble clay?

With aspirations like thine own,
Pure being, whom we dare not mourn,
O let us mark, where dwells "no night,"
A new-born, active, burning light.

Shine on for ever, tranquil star!
Though in far heaven thy glories are,
Their solemn beams shall from this hour
Fall on our souls with added power.

Each thrilling cadence, each mild word
Of love or wisdom we have heard,
From gifted lips now still and cold,
Shall be imbued with power untold.

Go, Christian sage! Death now hath wrought
On pages glowing with thy thought;
Death, who hath calmed all pain, hath sealed
Thy power on earth, — and heaven revealed.

DEATH.

WRITTEN AFTER READING DR. BRAZER'S SERMON ON THE DEATH OF HONORABLE LEVERETT SALTONSTALL.

C. J. FOX.

And is this death? His suffering o'er,
Is this but lifeless clay?
Stands the freed soul before the throne
Of endless day?

O human life! mysterious soul!
Breath of the living God!
Its frame has now an angel's power,
Is now a clod!

So calm he lived, without complaint,
We scarce could think him ill;
And the same look he wore in life
Is on him still.

His heart replete with Christian grace
    Found joy in suffering;
To him the grave no victory had,
        And death no sting.

May I so live, that, when I feel
    Death knocking at my heart,
My faith may bid all fear "Be still!"
        As I depart.

A DEATH-BED.

JAMES ALDRICH.

Her suffering ended with the day,
  Yet lived she at its close,
And breathed the long, long night away,
  In statue-like repose.

But when the sun, in all his state,
  Illumed the eastern skies,
She passed through glory's morning gate,
  And walked in Paradise!

THE MARTYRDOM OF PERPETUA.

A. D. 202.

S. G. BULFINCH.

THERE sat within a dungeon's gloom
A female form of mournful grace.
Thoughts of her stern approaching doom
Had driven the rose-tint from her face.
Yet not for that, amid her woe,
Did her high heart its faith resign;
And that pale cheek at times would glow
With light, whose glory was divine.

They came, the dear ones of her hearth,
To whom her earthly love was given;
They strove to win again to earth
The spirit, ready now for heaven.
Husband and sister sued in vain,
In vain, though burning tears replied;
To love she gave those drops of pain,
Triumphant over all beside.

Her aged father came and knelt,
Bowed his white locks before his child;
And the sad daughter deeply felt,
Yet through her tears looked up and smi
They brought her infant; as he lay
Before her, in his slumber fair,

Almost the mother's heart gave way,
But God had heard his martyr's prayer.

Her strength arose. " My child shall be
Safe in thy sheltering care, my God!
I give him, this sad hour, to thee:
And when this dreadful path is trod,
May I not hope in robes of light
To hover o'er his slumbering head,
And o'er my father's locks of white
A spirit-daughter's blessing shed?"

She died; that spirit, calm and high,
Sustained her through the dreadful hour;
She died as those alone can die
Whom faith in God has girt with power.
To her own fearless heart, her hand
Guided the gladiator's sword.
Yet, through their grief, the Christian band
That night the hymn of triumph poured.

The pure, the faithful, was at rest;
For her a glorious crown was won,
And now in mansions of the blest
On that fair brow for ever shone.
And courage rose to meet their death
In those the Christians' path who trod;
And, won by her undaunted faith,
A thousand heathen turned to God.

SONNET.

1 CORINTHIANS XV.

GEORGE LUNT.

O fool, to judge that He who from the earth
   Created man, cannot his form restore!
   The scattered elements from every shore
Call back and clothe with a celestial birth!
See from its sheath the buried seed break forth
   Blade, stalk, leaf, bud, and now the perfect
         flower,
   Changing and yet the same, and of His power
A token each; and art thou counted worth
Less than the meanest herb? Changed from the
         dust,
   And little lower than the angels made,
   More changed by sin, to death itself betrayed,
Yet heir of heaven by an immortal trust.
Doubter unwise, in reason's narrow school,
Well might the great Apostle say, "Thou fool!"

A FUNERAL SONG.

FROM "THE FUNERAL DAY OF SIR WALTER SCOTT."

MRS. HEMANS.

Lowly and solemn be
Thy children's cry to thee,
        Father divine!
A hymn of suppliant breath,
Owning that life and death
        Alike are thine!

        A spirit on its way
Sceptred the earth to sway
        From thee was sent:
Now call'st thou back thine own,—
Hence is that radiance flown,
        To earth but lent.

Watching in breathless awe,
The bright head bowed we saw
        Beneath thy hand!
Filled by one hope, one fear,
Now o'er a brother's bier
        Weeping we stand.

How hath he passed,—the lord
Of each deep bosom chord,—
        To meet thy sight!

Unmantled and alone,
On thy blest mercy thrown,
    O Infinite!

So from his harvest home
Must the tired peasant come;
    So, in one trust,
Leader and king must yield
The naked soul, revealed
    To thee, All Just!

The sword of many a fight, —
What then shall be its might?
    The lofty lay
That rushed on eagle wing, —
What shall its memory bring?
    What hope, what stay?

O Father! in that hour,
When earth all succoring power
    Shall disavow, —
When spear, and shield, and crown
In faintness are cast down, —
    Sustain us, Thou!

By Him who bowed to take
The death-cup for our sake,
    The thorn, the rod, —
From whom the last dismay
Was not to pass away, —
    Aid us, O God!

Tremblers beside the grave,
We call on thee to save,
Father divine!
Hear, hear our suppliant breath,
Keep us, in life and death,
Thine, only thine!

THE ANGEL BY THE TOMB.

SARAH F. ADAMS.

The mourners came at break of day
Unto the garden sepulchre,
With darkened hearts, to weep and pray
For Him, the loved one buried there.
What radiant light dispels the gloom?
An angel sits beside the tomb.

The Earth doth mourn her treasures lost,
All sepulchred beneath the snow,
When wintry winds and chilling frost
Have laid her summer glories low:
The spring returns, the flowerets bloom,—
An angel sits beside the tomb.

Then mourn we not beloved dead;
E'en while we come to weep and pray,

The happy spirit far hath fled,
  To brighter realms of endless day:
    Immortal Hope dispels the gloom!
    An angel sits beside the tomb.

THE PAUPER'S DEATH-BED.

MRS. CAROLINE BOWLES SOUTHEY.

TREAD softly! bow the head, —
  In reverent silence bow!
No passing-bell doth toll,
Yet an immortal soul
  Is passing now.

Stranger! however great,
  With lowly reverence bow;
There 's one in that poor shed, —
One by that paltry bed,
  Greater than thou.

Beneath that beggar's roof,
  Lo! Death doth keep his state;
Enter, — no crowds attend;
Enter, — no guards defend
  This palace gate.

That pavement, damp and cold,
  No smiling courtiers tread;
One silent woman stands,
Lifting with meagre hands
  A dying head.

No mingling voices sound, —
  An infant wail alone;
A sob suppressed, — again
That short, deep gasp, — and then
  The parting groan!

O change! O wondrous change!
  Burst are the prison bars!
This moment there, so low,
So agonized, and now
  Beyond the stars!

O change! stupendous change!
  There lies the soulless clod:
The sun eternal breaks,
The new immortal wakes, —
  Wakes with his God.

THE PRESENCE OF THE DEPARTED.

HIRAM WITHINGTON.

"Are they not all ministering spirits?"

The sainted dead! think you they linger not,
Nor e'er to this lone world return again?
Say, do they not revisit each loved spot
Whose sight doth waken such a thrilling strain
Within our longing hearts? O, not in vain
They came and went! nor severed are those ties
That bound them to this life of joy and pain:
They come, — they come, — and bid our spirits rise,
And dwell in peace with them, beneath the heavenly skies!

They are about us; — as when Israel's flight
God's spirit guided through the desert's sand,
In cloud by day and fiery lamp by night,
And led in safety to the promised land, —
So round our path these guardian spirits stand,
To shield us 'mid temptation's fiery heat;
In sorrow's night to take us by the hand,
And lead us gently to that mercy-seat
Whence comes celestial light to guide our wandering feet.

They come, where, in life's weary hours of care,
The fainting heart is burdened, tempted, tried;
Bringing from heaven the strength to do and bear,
The Father's pitying mercy hath supplied;
Beneath our roof at evening they abide,
Like angel-guests whom Abraham fed of yore,
Through the night's stillness watching by our side,
Giving us visions of the world before, —
That world of tranquil rest where partings come no more.

God's ministers, they watch each step of ours,
The loved and lost that on life's morning smiled;
Amidst our sleeping and unconscious hours,
They speak within our hearts in accents mild;
And, as a mother soothes her fretful child,
With words of strength and peace our souls they cheer:
O, could we calm our earthly passions wild,
And see this spirit-host for ever near,
We ne'er could feel that all alone we wander here!

"CALL THEM FROM THE DEAD."

W. J. FOX.

Call them from the dead
For our eyes to see:
Prophet-bards, whose awful word
Shook the earth, "Thus saith the Lord,"
And made the idols flee; —
A glorious company!

Call them from the dead
For our eyes to see:
Sons of wisdom, song, and power,
Giving earth her richest dower,
And making nations free; —
A glorious company!

Call them from the dead
For our eyes to see:
Forms of beauty, love, and grace,
"Sunshine in the shady place,"
That made it life to be; —
A blessed company!

Call them from the dead, —
Vain the call will be;
But the hand of Death shall lay,
Like that of Christ, its healing clay
On eyes which then shall see
That glorious company!

"IT IS TOLD ME I MUST DIE."

WRITTEN BY RICHARD LANGHORNE, BEFORE HIS EXECUTION, UPON AN UNJUST CHARGE OF TREASON, IN THE REIGN OF CHARLES THE SECOND.

SARGENT'S SELECTION.

It is told me I must die:
O happy news!
Be glad, O my soul,
And rejoice in Jesus, the Saviour!
If he intended thy perdition
Would he have laid down his life for thee?
Would he have called thee with so much love,
And illuminated thee with the light of the Spirit?
Would he have given thee his cross,
And given thee shoulders to bear it with patience?

It is told me I must die:
O happy news!
Come on, my dearest soul!
Behold, thy Jesus calls thee!
He prayed for thee upon his cross;
There he extended his arms to receive thee;
There he bowed down his head to kiss thee;
There he opened his heart to give thee entrance;
There he gave up his life to purchase life for thee.

It is told me I must die:
O what happiness!

I am going
To the place of my rest;
To the land of the living;
To the haven of security;
To the kingdom of peace;
To the palace of my God;
To the nuptials of the Lamb;
To sit at the table of my King;
To feed on the bread of angels;
To see what no eye hath seen;
To hear what no ear hath heard;
To enjoy what the heart of man cannot comprehend.

O my Father!
O thou best of all fathers,
Have pity on the most wretched of all thy children!
I was lost, but by thy mercy found;
I was dead, but by thy grace am now raised again;
I was gone astray after vanity,
But I am now ready to appear before thee,
O my Father!
Come, now, in mercy, and receive thy child!
Give him thy kiss of peace;
Remit unto him all his sins;
Clothe him with thy nuptial robe;
Permit him to have a place at thy feast;
And forgive all those who are guilty of his death.

FOR COMFORT IN DEATH.

HERRICK.

In the hour of my distress,
When temptations me oppress,
And when I my sins confess,
Sweet Spirit, comfort me!

When I lie within my bed,
Sick in heart, and sick in head,
And with doubts disquieted,
Sweet Spirit, comfort me!

When the house doth sigh and weep,
And the world is drowned in sleep,
Yet mine eyes the watch do keep,
Sweet Spirit, comfort me!

When the passing-bell doth toll,
And the Furies, in a shoal,
Come to fright my parting soul,
Sweet Spirit, comfort me!

When, God knows, I 'm tost about,
Either with despair or doubt, —
Yet before the glass be out,
Sweet Spirit, comfort me!

When the Tempter me pursu'th
With the sins of all my youth,
And half damns me with untruth,
Sweet Spirit, comfort me!

When the judgment is revealed,
And that opened which was sealed,
When to Thee I have appealed,
Sweet Spirit, comfort me!

DAYS OF MY YOUTH.

ST. GEORGE TUCKER.

Days of my youth, ye have glided away;
Hairs of my youth, ye are frosted and gray;
Eyes of my youth, your keen sight is no more;
Cheeks of my youth, ye are furrowed all o'er;
Strength of my youth, all your vigor is gone;
Thoughts of my youth, your gay visions are flown.

Days of my youth, I wish not your recall;
Hairs of my youth, I 'm content ye should fall;
Eyes of my youth, ye much evil have seen;
Cheeks of my youth, bathed in tears ye have been;
Thoughts of my youth, ye have led me astray;
Strength of my youth, why lament your decay?

Days of my age, ye will shortly be past;
Pains of my age, yet awhile can ye last;
Joys of my age, in true wisdom delight;
Eyes of my age, be religion your light;
Thoughts of my age, dread ye not the cold sod;
Hopes of my age, be ye fixed on your God.

FAREWELL TO LIFE.

LINES WRITTEN BY KÖRNER, WHEN HE LAY DANGEROUSLY WOUNDED AND HELPLESS, IN A FOREST, EXPECTING TO DIE.

TRANSLATED BY DR. FOLLEN.

THIS smarting wound, — these lips so pale and chill! —
My heart, with faint and fainter beating, says,
I stand upon the borders of my days.
Amen! my God, I own thy holy will.
The golden dreams, that once my soul did fill,
The songs of mirth, become sepulchral lays.
Faith! faith! That truth which all my spirit sways,
Yonder, as here, must live within me still.
And what I held as sacred here below,
What I embraced with quick and youthful glow,

Whether I called it liberty, or love,
A seraph bright I see it stand above;
And as my senses slowly pass away,
A breath transports me to the realms of day.

A POET'S DYING HYMN.

MRS. HEMANS.

> Be mute who will, who can,
> Yet I will praise Thee with impassioned voice!
> Me didst thou constitute a priest of thine
> In such a temple as we now behold,
> Reared for thy presence; therefore am I bound
> To worship, here and everywhere.
>
> WORDSWORTH.

THE blue, deep, glorious heavens! I lift my eye,
And bless thee, O my God! that I have met
And owned thine image in the majesty
Of their calm temple still! — that never yet
There hath thy face been shrouded from my sight
By noontide blaze, or sweeping storm of night, —
I bless thee, O my God!

That now still clearer, from their pure expanse,
I see the mercy of thine aspect shine,
Touching death's features with a lovely glance
Of light, serenely, solemnly divine,

And lending to each holy star a ray
As of kind eyes, that woo my soul away, —
I bless thee, O my God!

That I have heard thy voice, nor been afraid,
In the earth's garden, — 'midst the mountains old,
And the low thrillings of the forest shade,
And the wild sounds of waters uncontrolled,
And upon many a desert plain and shore, —
No solitude, for there I felt *Thee* more, —
I bless thee, O my God!

And if thy spirit on thy child hath shed
The gift, the vision of the unsealed eye,
To pierce the mist o'er life's deep meanings spread,
To reach the hidden fountain urns that lie
Far in man's heart, — if I have kept it free
And pure, a consecration unto thee, —
I bless thee, O my God!

If my soul's utterance hath by thee been fraught
With an awakening power, — if thou hast made
Like the winged seed the breathings of my thought,
And by the swift winds bid them be conveyed
To lands of other lays, and there become
Native as early melodies of home, —
I bless thee, O my God!

Not for the brightness of a mortal wreath,
  Nor for a place 'midst kingly minstrels dead,
But that perchance a faint gale of thy breath,
  A still, small whisper in my song, hath led
One struggling spirit upwards to thy throne,
Or but one hope, one prayer, — for this alone
      I bless thee, O my God!

That I have loved, — that I have known the love
  Which troubles in the soul the tearful springs,
Yet with a coloring halo from above
  Tinges and glorifies all earthly things,
Whate'er its anguish or its woe may be,
Still weaving links for intercourse with thee, —
      I bless thee, O my God!

That by the passion of its deep distress,
  And by the o'erflowing of its mighty prayer,
And by the yearning of its tenderness,
  Too full for words upon their stream to bear,
I have been drawn still closer to thy shrine,
Well-spring of love, the unfathomed, the divine;
      I bless thee, O my God!

That hope hath ne'er my heart or song forsaken,
  High hope, which e'en from mystery, doubt, or
    dread,
Calmly, rejoicingly, the things hath taken
  Whereby its torchlight for the race was fed, —

That passing storms have only fanned the fire
Which pierced them still with its triumphant
 spire,—
 I bless thee, O my God!

Now art thou calling me in every gale,
 Each sound and token of the dying day;
Thou leavest me not, though early life grows
 pale;
 I am not darkly sinking to decay;
But hour by hour, my soul's dissolving shroud
Melts off to radiance, as a silvery cloud.
 I bless thee, O my God!

And if this earth, with all its choral streams,
 And crowning woods, and soft or solemn skies,
And mountain sanctuaries for poet's dreams,
 Be lovely still in my departing eyes,—
'T is not that fondly I would linger here,
But that thy footprints on its dust appear.
 I bless thee, O my God!

And that the tender shadowing I behold,
 The tracery veining every leaf and flower,
Of glories cast in more consummate mould,
 No longer vassals to the changeful hour,—
That life's last roses to my thoughts can bring
Rich visions of imperishable spring,—
 I bless thee, O my God.

Yes! the young vernal voices in the skies
  Woo me not back, but, wandering past mine
      ear,
Seem heralds of the eternal melodies,
  The spirit-music, imperturbed and clear;
The full of soul, yet passionate no more, —
Let *me* too, joining those pure strains, adore!
          I bless thee, O my God!

Now aid, sustain me still! — to thee I come.
  Make thou my dwelling where thy children are;
And for the hope of that immortal home,
  And for thy Son, the bright and morning star,
The sufferer and the victor-king of death,
I bless thee with my glad song's dying breath!
          I bless thee, O my God!

"LIVING OR DYING, LORD, I WOULD BE THINE."

PARAPHRASED FROM FÉNÉLON.

Living or dying, Lord, I would be thine!
      O what is life?
      A toil, a strife,
Were it not lighted by thy love divine.
      I ask not wealth, —
      I crave not health, —
Living or dying, Lord, I would be thine!

O what is death?
When the poor breath
In parting can the soul to thee resign;
While patient love
Her trust doth prove.
Living or dying, Lord, I would be thine!

Throughout my days,
Be constant praise
Uplift to thee from out this heart of mine:
So shall I be
Brought nearer thee.
Living or dying, Lord, I would be thine!

ON —— ——.

R. M. MILNES.

Gently supported on the ready aid
Of loving hands, whose little work of toil
Her grateful prodigality repaid
With all the benediction of her smile,
She turned her failing feet
To the soft-pillowed seat,
Dispensing kindly greetings all the while.

Before the tranquil beauty of her face
I bowed in spirit, thinking that she were

A suffering Angel, whom the special grace
Of God intrusted to our pious care,
That we might learn from her
The art to minister
To heavenly beings in seraphic air.

There seemed to lie a weight upon her brain
That ever pressed her blue-veined eyelids down,
But could not dim her lustrous eyes with pain,
Nor seam her forehead with the faintest frown
She was as she were proud,
So young, to be allowed
To follow Him who wore the thorny crown.

Nor was she sad, but over every mood
To which her lightly-pliant mind gave birth,
Gracefully changing, did a spirit brood
Of quiet gayety and serenest mirth ;
And thus her voice did flow
So beautifully low,
A stream whose music was no thing of earth.

Now long that instrument has ceased to sound
Now long that gracious form in earth has lain
Tended by nature only, and unwound
Are all those mingled threads of love and pain
So let me weep, and bend
My head and wait the end,
Knowing that God creates not thus in vain.

FRAGMENT FOUND IN A SKELETON-CASE.

ANONYMOUS.

Behold this ruin! 't is a skull,
Once of ethereal spirit full.
This narrow cell was life's retreat;
This space was thought's mysterious seat.
What beauteous pictures filled this spot!
What dreams of pleasure, long forgot!
Nor grief nor joy, nor hope nor fear,
Has left one trace or record here!

Beneath this mouldering canopy
Once shone the bright and busy eye.
Yet start not at that dismal void:
If social love that eye employed,
If with no lawless fire it gleamed,
But with the dew of kindness beamed,
That eye shall be for ever bright
When stars and suns have lost their light.

Here, in this silent cavern, hung
The ready, swift, and tuneful tongue.
If falsehood's honey it disdained,
And, where it could not praise, was chained,
If bold in virtue's cause it spoke,
Yet gentle concord never broke,

That tuneful tongue shall plead for thee
When death unveils eternity!

Say, did these fingers delve the mine
Or with its envied rubies shine?
To hew the rock or wear the gem
Can nothing now avail to them.
But if the page of truth they sought,
And comfort to the mourners brought,
These hands a richer meed shall claim
Than all that waits on wealth or fame!

Avails it whether bare or shod
Those feet the paths of duty trod?
If from the bowers of joy they sped
To soothe affliction's humble bed,
If grandeur's guilty bribe they spurned,
And home to virtue's lap returned,
Those feet with angels' wings shall vie,
And tread the palace of the sky!

WHITEFIELD'S REMAINS.*

MISS H. F. GOULD.

Ye sacred relics, not with foot profane
  Would I disturb the quiet of the dead.
Where, wrapped in shades and stillness, ye have
    lain
  Till more than half a century hath fled!

I have no vainly curious eye to see
  How strange the works of time and death ap-
    pear, —
To find the sentence of mortality,
  "Ashes to ashes," executed here.

Yet I from infancy have longed to look,
  For once, on you, then bid a long farewell;
Since 't was from you great Whitefield's spirit
    took
  Her flight to mansions where the blessed dwell!

Ye were her earthen vessel! — and ye bore
  That goodly treasure on, from clime to clime!
Ye were the fine-wrought texture that she wore,
  And gently dropped, as closed the scene of
    time.

---

* Deposited beneath the pulpit of the First Presbyterian Church in Newburyport, Mass.

Here, hallowed dust! thou still hast slumbered on,
While o'er thy rest the beauteous feet of those
Who brought salvation's news have stood, then gone,
Tired with life's journey, to the grave's repose.

And wilt thou linger yet, till he who stands
Above thee now, the Gospel to proclaim,
Has ceased to lift in prayer his holy hands,
And monumental marble speaks his name?

O wait not this! *— but go and sleep unseen,
Deep in the bosom of thy mother earth!
Let nature deck thy couch with living green,
Till, changed, the archangel's trump shall call thee forth!

And now, farewell! I have been told by thee
The things a thousand tongues would fail to say:
Thou bidst the mortal part its value see,—
The soul mount up where WHITEFIELD's led the way!

* The removal of these remains to the public burial-ground was contemplated at the time this was written.

THE END.

www.ingramcontent.com/pod-product-compliance
Lightning Source LLC
LaVergne TN
LVHW010150110826
845151LV00002B/480